THE GOD WHO CHANGES LIVES
Volume Four

The God Who Changes Lives

Volume Four

Edited by Mark Elsdon-Dew

ALPHA INTERNATIONAL
LONDON

Unless otherwise indicated, biblical quotations are from either
the Good News Version © 1976, Second Edition 1994
by the American Bible Society; or the
New International Version, © 1973, 1978, 1984
by the International Bible Society.

ISBN 1 904074 56 1

Editor's acknowledgements

This book depends wholly upon the goodwill of its
contributors who not only agreed to be interviewed at length,
but then checked and re-checked the text. I am enormously
grateful to each of them.

We have had an amazing team involved in the book's
production. I would particularly like to thank Ana Lehmann
who, as well as interviewing two of the contributors,
masterminded the project from the start; and Oliver Ryder
who conducted several of the interviews. Finally, thanks
go as always to Sharon Hayles who is central to everything
we produce.

Published by Alpha International
Holy Trinity Brompton
Brompton Road, London, SW7 1JA

Contents

'Write down for the coming generation what the Lord has done, so that people not yet born will praise him.'

Psalm 102:18

Alpha

Many of the contributors to this book make particular reference to the Alpha course, a practical introduction to the Christian faith which has had a remarkable impact on many people's lives. The course has proved so popular that there are now more than 8,000 courses running in the UK and 28,000 courses running around the world.

Introduction

by Mark Elsdon-Dew

More than 10 years have passed since we first published a series entitled 'Holy Ghost Stories' on the back page of Holy Trinity Brompton's monthly church newspaper Focus.

A few years later, in 1995, a collection of those articles found their way into a book which we called *The God Who Changes Lives*. Somehow, the power and the love of God to transform people's lives – whatever situations they found themselves in – came through in that small volume.

Since then, we have published two further volumes of British stories and a collection of American ones in the same vein. Here is the fourth British volume – and the stories remind us that Jesus Christ offers new hope to today's generation just as he did to those of the past.

With the extraordinary growth of the Alpha course during the last decade, an increasing number of the stories in these books are about people who have come into a relationship with God through an experience of the course.

Throughout the series, the two questions I have asked myself when considering whether to include a story have remained the same. They are:

1. Is the person telling the story someone whose current

lifestyle is such that I can trust their account – and stable enough not to be rocked by the very act of telling their story publicly?

2. Is the story unusual enough, yet real enough, to prompt the reader to accept that something unusual took place which could possibly be put down to the presence of the living God?

I am most grateful to all the contributors who have allowed their stories to be told in this book. For many it has required great courage to allow sensitive areas of their lives to be laid bare. But they have gone ahead so that others may come to know the love of Jesus Christ for themselves.

In Psalm 145 the psalmist praises God saying, 'What you have done will be praised from one generation to the next.' Everyone whose story is told in this book feels the same way.

Holy Trinity Brompton, 2004

1

'I just sat on this bench drinking and drinking . . . kids used to spit at me and throw things at me.'

The story of Gram Seed

> *For three years Gram Seed lived day and night on a bench outside a small shopping arcade in Middlesbrough. In 1996, he lay close to death and God intervened in an extraordinary way . . .*

I was brought up by my grandparents – and for many years I didn't know why. When I was nine, my grandad told me that my dad was quite violent and used to beat my mum up. My nana was quite ill and suffered from depression a lot. In Middlesbrough we have a local mental institution called Saint Luke's, and my nana was a day patient there all her life. She went to that hospital every day apart from the weekends, and sometimes she would go in for months. They would give her terrible electric treatments and I would hate to see the effect they would have on her. It really was barbaric and they don't do it now.

When I was eight, my mum got married to another fellow and moved out to a house about two miles away. It was never suggested that I would go and live with them, so I stayed with my nana and grandad, who I loved. I felt that the new fellow never wanted me as part of the deal. As I grew up, I remember noticing that everyone else seemed to have mums and dads and brothers and sisters and stuff. It made me feel a bit of a freak, particularly as I knew other people thought of us as a bit like the Addams Family. My nana was a bit of a drinker and used to keep 24-pack cans of lager under her bed. When I was about ten, I nicked one of her cans and drank it. Then I went out for a walk and had a fag. As I was walking down the park, this bully from another estate who was about three years older than me tried to get some fags off me. I was really angry and I punched him. He hit the floor and then ran off. But the next day I noticed that everyone was talking to me and including me far more. I thought, 'Why does everyone want to knock about with me now? It must be because I hit that kid. So from then on I started fighting a lot. My uncle Terry was absolutely mad on Bruce Lee and I used to watch the films with him. I would practise the moves and became a really keen boxer as well.

From about the age of 12, I became a skinhead and started breaking into schools and nicking stuff. I started with my own school, nicking the saws, screwdrivers and stuff. Then I moved on to other schools and youth clubs. We would go through the windows, opening them from the outside with a piece of wire. Then at the weekend we would sell anything we took. I was treated as quite a madman because I wouldn't let anyone close to me. I grew up learning never to be afraid of anything, and would fight a lot with anyone on the street. My muscles were starting to come out and I was getting bigger and bigger. When I was about 14-years-old, I started hanging out with these lads from another estate who took magic mushrooms, which they picked off the hill nearby. They make you hallucinate and do strange things.

When I was 15 I was charged with 22 offences of burgling schools and youth clubs – but I had done many more than that. Me and the lads – three of us – would do it every night. We even stole cars – although we couldn't really drive. We wouldn't burgle houses, though. A few months later, while I was on bail, I was involved in a fight on a bus with another gang. There were about 50 of us in all – including punks and skinheads – when suddenly the bus started moving and we all thought it was time to get off in case the police came. As we leapt off, one lad from the other gang accidentally slipped under the wheels of the bus and was killed. That night the police came to arrest me and said, 'We're charging you with murder.' But I wasn't the only suspect and in the end no one was charged with that.

Nevertheless, I was classed as one of the hardest lads of my age in Middlesbrough. I was known as a bit of a psycho as I was not scared of anyone. I was sentenced to nine months in a detention centre for the burglaries – and served seven months – but little changed after I was out. I just went back to the same old lifestyle. Soon after I came out of prison, my grandad died of a massive heart attack and the family just fell to bits. He had gone into hospital for an operation and I never even went to visit him. I was just too consumed with my own life. When he died, I was really tortured, because I felt I had let him down by being in trouble all my life. At the same time, a lot of the family blamed me for putting pressure on him.

After that, they sold our nana's house and I had nowhere to live. I started living in loads of different places. By then, I had got introduced to fighting at football matches. I was never very interested in football because I thought it was for wimps, but then this kid said to me, 'Yeah, but there's lots of fighting and that.' So I thought, 'I'll come to that.' And I thought it was great. Middlesbrough were in the first division then and I would go every Saturday – or sometimes Tuesday nights. It was at football that I got slashed across the face with a knife, had a bottle stuck in my eye and chin, got four of my teeth knocked out, and got another big scar on my left arm from a police Alsatian dog.

I went to live in St Hilda's – an area of Middlesbrough known as 'over the border' – one of the roughest parts, with a family called the Wards. My nana moved in with my mum, but I never went because I didn't really get on with my stepdad and I don't think they wanted me there. I knew my nana loved me, but she was very ill. She would give me money and that on a weekend. By then I wouldn't let anyone get close to me, no one – even though I would pick up loads of lassies all the time. I got quite good at robbing – nicking stuff like tellies out of the back of lorries or all the cigarettes out of clubs. A year later I had enough to buy my own house in Middlesbrough. I was bang in the middle of organised crime in Middlesbrough. I was selling counterfeit perfume, counterfeit Lacoste tracksuits, counterfeit Lacoste T-shirts, counterfeit money, and all kinds. I was right in the middle of it all. I always seemed to have like loads of money – I had gold rings on every finger, Rolex watch, Giorgio Armani suits – but I would squander it. I would smoke cannabis all the time and would often be off my head with drugs.

When I was 19, I was staying at my mum's overnight when my nana died. It was a terrible shock, but it was made worse because my nana's wallet went missing at the time. Every single person thought I nicked it and I must have scared her and that's why she died. It was all completely untrue, but when the police wanted to interview me, I just got completely drunk. In the middle of the night I caused a bit of a commotion by waking up everyone in my mum and stepdad's house. My stepdad was furious, so I hit him. After that, I started smashing the house up by hitting the walls and smashing my fists through the doors. I was taken away by the police. My mum and stepdad got an injunction out on me, banning me not only from their house but the whole village where they lived.

Soon after that I got into a fight with the police at a football match and got two years in prison, where I served 11 months. I was totally off my head on drink and drugs when it happened. They smashed up my house, pulling up the floorboards and everything, searching for evidence, and the house ended up being sold. I came out of prison just before my 21st birthday and made a bit of a pact with our mum again. She gave a great birthday party for me in Middlesbrough for my 21st birthday, but I had nowhere to live. I was a big bloke by now – six foot five with a 62-inch chest and 21-inch biceps. I had been training all my life and was muscley – I weighed 21 stone.

After that, I was basically sleeping anywhere I could for a night and needed money, so I was soon back involved in crime and stuff. That meant time in jail, where I spent a lot of the next years. I was always fighting in jail, and often with prison officers – anyone who stood for authority. That meant time in solitary confinement, where I would get beaten up by the officers. That was how I got more of my teeth knocked out. While in solitary, I used to 'smoke the Bible' – using the paper for rollies, you got to smoke it. I used to shave my head bald, totally bald, because you weren't allowed to have your head shaved bald. You also had to have your shirt collar down, your top button fastened and your shirt tucked in, so I would put my collar up and pull my shirt out. They used to tell me to put it back in and I wouldn't – so I would go to my cell. Then the next time I'd be let out of my cell I'd 'kick off', which meant I'd throw my dinner at them or kick the servery over with all the food on it. Then they shut you in solitary. When you are let out, you go to the governor, and he'd say, 'Right, I'm going to add 30 days on to your prison sentence.'

I'd say, 'So what?' and would walk away.

At that, he'd say, 'I'm not going to be abused.'

I'd say, 'Well you are, because I'm going to make your life hell.' And I did make their lives hell while I was in there. I just hated them.

In 1990, I got out of jail again and got a job as a doorman in a night club. It was hard work, but it kept me out of trouble . . . until New Year's Day 1991. A fight broke out on the dance floor of the club and I moved in. What I didn't know was that two undercover coppers were circulating the pubs and clubs that night – and I hit one of them hard and he went down. I had no idea he was a copper. It could only happen to me. I just put my hands up and said, 'Look, I didn't know they were coppers. I thought it was the best thing to do, you know.' I got 12 months for that. I did 6 months out of the 12 and when I came out I decided to end it all. I sat down on a bench near an arcade of shops in Middlesbrough one night, and I took out my knife with a 12-inch blade and cut my wrists. I woke up in hospital with a copper sitting next to me. The police had actually thought someone was trying to murder me – but I didn't know that. So when I saw the copper, I pulled the drip out and legged it.

I was later found and put into the mental institution, St Luke's – the same place my nana had been in. By now I was hearing voices and stuff and drinking cider and generally becoming more and more of a bum. When I came out of St Luke's in 1993, the council gave me a flat near the bench where I had cut my wrists – but I didn't want to live in it. By now I was just sick of life – totally sick of it. I didn't want to leave St Luke's because I'd already been acclimatised to it – not having any pressure. So at the end of 1993, I decided to stay on my bench and just drink myself to death. I also injected heroin, sniffed cocaine, sniffed paracetamol, drank meths . . . I just sat on this bench drinking and drinking and drinking. For a long while I just wore a T-shirt – in the cold and rain and snow and frost with just a T-shirt. Then one of the lads in the town (called Dale) came up to me one Christmas and said, 'What's happened to you, my friend?' and all that. Then he gave me twenty quid and put a £250 jacket around me – which I went and sold for another twenty quid.

I stayed on that bench day and night until 1996 – apart from the odd night when I would go to my flat to warm up. But the prostitutes would use my flat for their business, so there were always people there. Kids used to spit at me and throw things at me and slap my head around and flick fags at me. I'd become a tramp. I used to poo myself and wee myself. I was just a stench. I talked to myself the whole time. I would beg and people would give me pound coins and other cash, but otherwise no one would bother with me. I was a chronic alcoholic and I was ready to die. I used to drink 28 to 30 pints of White Lightning every day, which I could afford because of my begging. I even stole from the collection plate at the back of one of the churches to pay for my drinking.

It was one night in March 1996 that a group of around eight people came along and they were talking to the prostitutes and that. I was on my bench and two of the lads came over to me. One said, 'I just want to tell you Jesus loves you.'

I said, 'What?' and started swearing at him and telling him to go away. And they went away.

The next Friday they came back and said, 'Look, Jesus loves you, really, you know.' I told them to get away again and said I didn't want to know about Jesus. They seemed to have this type of boldness about them as though they weren't really scared. But I think they were wary of me. After that, I started seeing these lads everywhere I went. Everywhere. I'd never seen them before. I would walk from my bench through the town and suddenly one of them would say, 'Hey Gram, how are you doing?' Sometimes they would give me a lift in a car if I wanted to go and see one of my mates in a pub. I would often go and see them on pay-day, because I knew they'd look after me.

One night I burned my leg quite badly on the electric fire in my flat because I fell asleep against the bar. These Christians, Peter and Aiden, came up to me on the bench later and said, 'Gram, have you seen your leg?' They took me to hospital, but when the nurse looked at me she said, 'The worst thing we're going to have to do is to surgically remove your socks.' I had worn the socks for five or six months without changing them, and my skin had grown over my socks. In the end, they could only take them off with a scalpel. I went back to the bench but some time later, in late 1996, I collapsed in the flat and no one could wake me. They called the ambulance and when I got to the hospital, they found I had septicaemia, pneumonia, hypothermia, severe malnutrition, severe dehydration and my liver and kidneys had failed (apart from that I was OK!).

I was in a coma and on the fifth night of the coma they got my mother into a room with my stepdad and said, 'As his only legal guardian, we are advising you to allow us to switch the ventilation machine off that's keeping him breathing, because there's nothing we can do for him now.'

She thought about it and said, 'Look, I want you to keep trying – at least till you've got some more proof.'

Two hours later they took my mum back into this room and said, 'We've tried some more tests on your son and he's still not responding. We've tried to get him to respond to treatment for five days, and he isn't. There's no oxygen in his blood, and the short of it is that even if he wakes up, he's going to be paralysed from the neck down. It is only the machine that is keeping him breathing.'

And my mum said, 'I don't care. You fight for him. There's breath there – keep fighting.'

The following day, the Christian lads, Pete and Aiden and the others, arrived at the hospital. They had missed me on my bench and had been asking around about what had happened to me. So they came to the hospital and asked my mother what happened. She told them and they said, 'Can we pray for him?'

Mum said, 'Yeah, of course. I don't know what you mean by "pray for him", but go for it.'

So they put their hands on me and said, 'In the name of Jesus Christ of Nazareth, give this man new life.'

And I woke up. My eyes opened at once and I started breathing by myself. I slipped back to sleep, but I stayed breathing on my own after that. It was after another two days that I woke up and I said to my mum, 'What happened?'

She said, 'These lads prayed for you.'

I said, 'Who did they pray to?'

'God.'

'God?!'

'Yes, Jesus.'

And I said, 'What does Jesus want to know about a scumbag like me for? I thought he only liked nice people who went to church and didn't swear and spit and fight.'

She said, 'I don't know son, you'd better ask them. They'll be back later. They've been in every day since they found out you were in here.'

So when the lads came in, I asked them and they told me about Jesus coming and dying on a cross so that I could be forgiven. I remember pulling the sheets up and laughing. They kept coming as long as I was in hospital and they never pushed it about Christianity. They used to just come and sit with me and chat with me. And I used to think it was great. When I got out of hospital, I couldn't walk properly. I had two walking sticks and had to go downstairs on my bum. I was really weak. I got a room with one of my old friends – but I still saw quite a bit of the Christian lads, who would come and visit. I would often ask them questions about this Jesus.

Then one day one of them said, 'Look, you're asking loads of questions. Why don't you come on an Alpha course at our church?' He explained it was a course where you could ask all these kinds of questions. I thought, 'Church? You're joking, aren't you?' But in the end I agreed to give it a try. So I went to Alpha and there were about 60 people in this room – young and old – and I thought, 'What a load of rubbish – but at least the food's good.' At the group, they seemed to be just talking a lot of rubbish about this Jesus fellow and I was swearing – just having a laugh at them. The following Wednesday I went back and it seemed a bit easier. I was still swearing and felt like I had nothing to say. At one point, I left the room and wandered down this corridor looking for the safe, because I thought I would take the money. I came to a locked door and thought, 'Shall I get my knife out and open the door?' Then I thought, 'Nah, I'll leave it' and I went back to the group. By now, I was really cleaned up and friends had given me nice clothes and even paid for a haircut. I felt really great and even started looking forward to Wednesdays, because it was a night out and I felt good. I remember saying to a friend called Lizzie, 'I think I should see a psychiatrist.'

She said, 'Why?'

I said, 'Well, you know this Christian place? I've just had a bath and a shave and I can't wait to get there.'

She said, 'Ah, it'll go. It'll pass. Don't worry. It's just a new thing. You'll get there tonight and then the next week it'll wear off. Don't worry about it.' By now, I didn't want to swear when I was at Alpha because I could see these were nice people – but I couldn't stop, however hard I tried.

One night after Alpha, one of the Christian guys, Martin, said, 'Why don't you come back to my house tonight and meet my wife and have a coffee and a cake and that?' So I went back and was there till half twelve that night – just talking. Martin wasn't bothered about me swearing and his wife wasn't bothered about me swearing. I couldn't stop. Then came the Alpha Day Away. I was in two minds whether to go or not, but I thought, 'It's a day out anyway – and all the group's going and there'll be loads of food.' We listened to these talks about the Holy Spirit and that afternoon – it was a quarter to three on November 9, 1996 – Martin, who was leading, said, 'If you want to receive a gift, it's normal to put your hands out . . .' He explained that it was sometimes the same with receiving the Holy Spirit. Then he invited the Spirit to come.

I put my hands out and I remember saying to Jesus, 'Jesus, if this is real, if it's true what these lads have said – that you love me – then prove it. I want you to prove it to me.' And I just felt this indescribable love surging into my heart. I just got this love. It was all over me. I sat down and I was crying. I was really weeping – and I'd never cried for anyone, not even when my nana and grandad died. It was a weakness, crying. I mean, I cried when I was drunk – many times – when a leaf fell off a tree or a cat crossed the road. But if you're drunk then you cry about everything. But this time I was sober and I was weeping. I was just saying to God, 'Thank you. Thank you.' I just felt so wanted, so needed. Then Martin led me in a prayer, when I said, 'Dear Jesus, I acknowledge that you died for me. Please forgive me for not acknowledging you all my life and just ignoring you. Please come into my life and keep me free for ever. Amen.'

I felt I belonged to someone at last. All my life I'd never belonged to anyone. I was a misfit and here I was belonging to someone. That night, I got home and said to my Christian friend, 'Peter, you must take me to the centre of Middlesbrough, I have to tell the prostitutes and the heroin addicts about Jesus, because he's real.' And that Saturday night, I went out and told them all. I think they thought I was brain damaged. And do you know what else happened that day? I stopped swearing. It went – disappeared. To this day I've never sworn again. I don't even think about swearing. Jesus just took it away. Lying in bed that night, I prayed, 'Jesus, I know you are real and that you died for me. From now on, every single day of my life, I'm going to go and tell everyone about you.' I felt totally clean, totally washed. The following day, I went to church. I was very weak still, but I was getting better and better. Even my insides were all starting to work again.

My whole life started changing at once. Although I drank a vast amount and smoked like a chimney up until that day, I have never drunk or smoked a fag since. I finished the Alpha course and became a helper on the next one. And the more I did it, and the more I spent time with Christians, I just had this strong urge to love Jesus more, and to tell people more. Jesus was now my friend. I started praying regularly and although I couldn't read properly – and still can't – I still wanted to read the Bible and now have a large-print Bible. There is a scripture which says, 'Those who are forgiven much will love much' and it is true. I love everybody now. I never loved my mum or my stepdad, but I love them now. Because of the forgiveness that Jesus has given me, he has put a new love for people in my heart.

For years I sat on that bench thinking, 'I want to die, I want to die.' But now all I want to do is live because of what Jesus has done for me. It's just totally the opposite.

In 1999, Gram Seed married Natasha, whom he had met on a Christian training course. They now have two sons, Caleb and Boaz. Gram visits prisons on a regular basis to help with Alpha courses and to tell prisoners about Jesus Christ. He says, 'When you can see no light there is only darkness to walk in. That's why I felt the need to fill my life with violence, drink and drugs. When Jesus woke me from that coma in August 1996, my life was headed in another direction. On 9 November 1996 at 2.45pm, the eyes of my heart were opened to the light of the world. I have hope and a life worth living for every day, not just today. My family – Natasha, Caleb and Boaz – are the greatest joy, next to Jesus.'

'I came to accept violence as part of my life.'

The story of Ross Mockeridge

> *Martial arts black belt Ross Mockeridge, from south east London, was living a violent lifestyle working as a bouncer on nightclub doors. He was frustrated with his life. Here he describes how a leaflet through his door paved the way to a series of profound changes:*

I come from a caring family background with loving parents. I have one older brother – and I think that was where the difficulties for me started. His name is Garry and he was successful at everything he turned his hand to. He was top of the class in a whole range of different subjects, and he played in the school rugby and cricket teams. He played junior cricket for Kent and basically everything that he touched turned to gold. Mum and Dad were of course very proud of his fantastic achievements – and I think they and my teachers were expectant of me too. But by contrast I was a little bit below average academically, and although I made the cricket team, I was never in his class.

While he went on to university, I left school at 16 because I couldn't stand it. I was comparing myself to him all the time. I had this feeling of struggling to keep up with him, and it was not possible for me. After leaving school, I drifted from job to job with no direction in life. I worked in a couple of shops and sports centres. One of my main interests was martial arts, and I kept going with that after leaving school. Over the years I got black belts in Judo, Jujitsu, Kung Fu and in two forms of Sambo – one in sport and one in combat. One day a friend of mine said, 'You could look after yourself pretty well. Why don't you get some work on night-club doors? It is far better money than what you're earning at the moment.' I thought, 'Well, he's right.' I thought it would be a step up the ladder financially.

Getting a job was pretty easy with my background, and my first night was at the Astoria in Charing Cross Road – a very, very large, well-known nightclub with a capacity of maybe 3,000. They have live acts there. People like Kylie Minogue have appeared on centre stage there – it is a big club. There are around 25 on the door. That first night went well enough and I started going around to different nightclubs. I have worked in Astoria, Adrenalin Village, Oxygen, Leisure Lounge, Fuel – all in the West End.

The job is mainly to act as a peace keeper, making sure that trouble makers don't enter the premises. To do this, you have to make a very quick assessment as they are approaching the door. My policy would be to engage them in a little bit of a conversation – get a little bit of a feel for them. I'd say 'Hi guys, how many of you are there?' If they looked very rough or you could tell they'd been drinking, that was a definite refusal. It's a lot better to deal with trouble on the door than to deal with trouble inside the club. Inside, it is a question of policing the place – looking out for anyone who might be drinking too much or selling drugs. Drugs are very prevalent throughout the club world. Drug selling and club culture go hand in hand. Ecstasy is the main one, but there's cocaine – or 'Charlie', as it's known.

The first time violence came my way was when I was working in a club called Venoms. I was on the door and two guys didn't like being refused and a fight ensued. They went down. Since then I've been in many, many violent situations. Once I nearly lost my life on the door. I was in Covent Garden and a colleague of mine started swapping words with a great big Australian guy. I tried to calm the situation down when the man's girlfriend got hysterical and started attacking my friend. So I just pulled the girl off, not hard but firmly. At this great big boyfriend – who was about 6'5" or so – just punched me right in the face. I got into him and we went down onto the floor. I got on top of him and hit him a couple of times so he was bloodied up a bit. Then I stopped. But unbeknownst to me his girlfriend had got a great big metal rope hold and was aiming to hit me over the back of my head with it. As she swung it towards my head, my friend just got to her in time before it hit me. If she had hit my head it could quite easily have killed me, or at the very least fractured my skull. There have been many similar violent situations.

I think there's a certain culture – certainly among young

men – which involves a time of binge drinking in the pub until 11 o'clock, and then off to the nightclub to try to get in there. So we are left dealing with people who have already been drinking too much. We then refuse them entry and they don't like to be refused entry. Hence you get problems – and unless you employ violence against them, they will use violence on you. I'm not a big guy and my usual tactic was to use what in Jujitsu is called a 'strangle' around the neck. It's quite frightening for the person because they can actually pass out. It cuts all the oxygen supply to the brain off and they pass out from that. I have passed people out with it. They're only out for a few seconds and then they come around usually with no ill effects.

I think over the years I had at least one type of incident every fortnight. I came to accept violence as part of my life. In the end I became de-sensitised to it and I was aware of it eating away inside me, because hurting someone is not a pleasurable thing at all. I had a lot of anger inside me. That anger expressed itself through the violence, but I hated myself for doing it. Inside the clubs there was a lot of promiscuity. Sometimes they would have sex in the club toilets or outside the club there and then. The gay scene is quite big in the club world, and if you were working a gay night it was very, very common for these guys to immediately hook up with a stranger and go off in a darkened corner or under the stage somewhere, and commit a lewd act. There is also a lot of drug taking and selling – often linked to organised crime. So if you go and stop a dealer it could well be that he's got some very, very shady people behind him.

There is a certain stigma attached to bouncers. But like any profession you've got good and bad elements. In the bouncing world you have got quite a few rotten apples.

You've got people that will go far beyond what is required to stop a person. You've also got doormen that actively take part in the sale of drugs within the club, and they're making good money on the side through people selling the drugs and so forth. I was questioned quite a few times by the police about assaults – bouncers have not got a good reputation – but I was never charged. I was lucky not to have been involved in something like a charge or a court case. It's very, very difficult to be involved in violence week in, week out, without having that happen. Throughout all this time I was living in my own little flat in Grove Park, south east London. I was doing quite a lot of amateur wrestling, and won the British championships at Sambo wrestling in 1997 and Kurash wrestling in 1999.

One day in mid-1999 I went out shopping and, when I got back home at lunchtime, I found a leaflet on the doormat. It had been pushed through my letterbox. It was about something called the Alpha course, which was described as a course in basic Christianity. At the time I was depressed and frustrated with life. I thought life had no meaning – and my life certainly had no direction, no purpose, and no substance. It was just an existence. It wasn't what I would call living. I'd never heard of Alpha, but I had this yearning for something more. As I looked at the leaflet I had a kind of inward battle: 'Shall I, shan't I? What will I get out of it? I'm not too sure about this . . .' I lived opposite a church called St Mildred's, but I would never have had the guts to take myself inside as a total stranger, of my own volition. But two weeks later, when the Monday night of Alpha came along, I thought to myself, 'Right, I'm going to go.'

I got right up to the church door and I almost balked at that point. In the end I thought, 'Oh, come on. Let's just see what it's like.' I walked through the door and I received a very, very warm welcome. It made all the difference. It turned out to be a man called David Nicholls, who was very much the opposite of me. He works in the city, has a great job, family, etc. He is quite a bit older than me. He welcomed me with a very warm smile. I said, 'Excuse me, is this the right place for the Alpha course?'

He said, 'Yes, yes.' Then he said, 'Would you like a cup of tea?' He took me over to get a cup of tea and then stayed with me and talked to me a little bit.

I found it all a bit daunting. There were about 20 people there and we watched the video. At the end I thought, 'I'll come back next week and see what happens.' It didn't move any mountains for me. I went the following week, and then the next, and I became more and more impressed with it. The people were really nice and the talks were great. I think I was the only one who had a sort of violent background. Most of the other people were ordinary people who did general office work. But Nicky's talks [Nicky Gumbel, the Alpha course speaker] did so much for me, but it was a gradual process. By about the fourth week of the course I was becoming really convinced. It was the Alpha night and I prayed to God a prayer I found in the booklet called, *Why Jesus?* I just thanked Jesus for dying for me and for acting as my Saviour. I repented of my sins and asked God to come into my life. I didn't feel anything in particular, but was glad I had said it.

A short time after that we went down to a little church in Bromley for the Alpha Day Away. It would be fair to say that I was looking forward to it. One of the leaders had said, 'Come prepared for something special,' but I just thought to myself, 'Yeah, yeah. Nothing's going to happen.' On the day we had the talks on the Holy Spirit, and then the leaders, David and Kay, said they were going to invite the Holy Spirit to come. At that time I was leaning forward in prayer. They laid their hands on me and asked the Holy Spirit to come. I didn't really think anything was going to happen at all. I was completely and utterly amazed by what happened. I'm not normally given to any kind of fantasy or emotion or anything, but I felt this great heat come on my head and down on my right shoulder blade and a little on my left. There was an intense feeling of power. The next thing I knew I was just in tears. I don't know why, but the tears were flowing liberally down my face and I thought, 'What am I doing?'

It was a life changing experience for me. The sessions up to that point had been getting better and better. I was becoming more and more encouraged. But it was the Alpha Day Away that was the straw that broke the camel's back. I wasn't an emotional type of guy in any way, shape or form. In fact I think I learnt to bottle up my emotions because of my experiences on the door. It was very important on the doors not to show any emotion. The Alpha course made such a difference to me. I made some really special friendships on that course and, ever since, things have been getting better and better. I started going along to Sunday services soon after starting the course, and it is a wonderful church. They are just so full of the Holy Spirit and have got so much love to give to you. I immediately felt their warmth.

One of the first changes was to my language. It was a real problem for me because I would swear in almost every sentence. It was part of my vocabulary. After I did Alpha I made a conscious effort to try and stop using these bad words. It was very difficult because it was a kind of addiction, but it got to the stage that if I said a swear word I would immediately hurt inside, because I felt I was hurting Jesus. I don't swear at all now. I started praying and reading the Bible regularly. I have read all through the New Testament, and sometimes it brought tears to my eyes when I saw what Jesus did, and how he healed people and how he came to save us.

After Alpha I was at complete pains to avoid any sort of confrontation on the doors. I really would do my utmost in terms of trying to de-escalate and calm the situation down. I was baptised in February 2002 – and it was around that time that I decided I didn't want to be involved in the 'doors scene' any more. I just had too much love inside me – too much love for God and, to be honest, for other people as well. I had grown up with martial arts all my life and had my teaching licences, so I thought I would have a go at making a business of it. Now I run classes and also teach people as a personal trainer on a one-to-one basis.

Before Alpha I never really thought of Jesus as God. But now he's my Lord, he's my Saviour. He's everything to me. I can't begin to tell you what Jesus means to me. He's everything. I love him with all my heart.

Ross Mockeridge continues to attend St Mildred's Church in Lee, South London. He runs his own business teaching martial arts.

2

'She said, "Get out now. You're in deep trouble." '

The story of Christine Woodall

For over ten years, at various intervals, Christine Woodall, from Guernsey, became more and more involved in astrology, 'spiritual healing' and communicating with the dead. Then a Christian friend invited her to a local church group, where she attended an Alpha course. Here she describes what happened:

I am a Guernsey person and I was brought up in Guernsey. I went to a local Catholic church every week with my mum and dad and my younger brother and sister. I found it quite boring and I used to count the words on the mass sheet to pass the time.

I always used to have the same list of sins when I went to confession, telling the priest stories about hitting my brother and being horrible to my mum. I never understood it then, it just made me anxious. I went to a Catholic school which involved a lot of hymn singing in the mornings. The ones I mostly remember were all about blood, which was a bit depressing. When I was 17 I went to Bath University to study French and German, and I kept going to church off and on throughout my time there, because I thought I ought to. I had this feeling that if I didn't go I was letting my dad down – it was very important to him.

At the end of university I married Mark, who was on the same course as me. Although he was an atheist we got married at my Catholic church in Guernsey in 1984. He did it because that was what I wanted. I carried on going to church, but in 1989 we moved to Portugal. We were there for three years, but I only went to church a couple of times. I just couldn't be bothered. Instead, I became very interested in the whole business of hands-on healing. I read books on the subject – not in a Christian context, but to do with harnessing the energy of the atmosphere through your hands. I did a correspondence course in astrology. I learned all the calculations – all to do with the precise minute and the place of a person's birth, taking into account different time zones and everything. I also learned about the different interpretations of the planets and signs, etc.

During our time in Portugal I got pregnant, and so we decided to come back to Guernsey. Once back, my dad asked me every week if I wanted to go to church and I said I didn't. I just didn't want to get involved again. When William was born we got him baptised when he was ten days old. It was important because being a Catholic was like a nationality to me rather than a religion.

Right from the time I moved back to the island, everywhere I went I seemed to meet Christians – mostly from a non-denominational church on the island called King's Church. When William was 15 months old I did a first aid course where I met someone called Mandy Hayter. I gradually found out that she was a Christian and went to King's Church. I also went to a toddler group and met somebody else who went to the same church. I then started selling books by party plan with somebody else who went to that church and I thought, 'Oh God, not another one.' They were friendly and quite outgoing so we used to find plenty to talk about – but I didn't ask any questions about religion, I didn't want to get involved.

One day I was looking through the local paper when I saw a little advert for something called a 'healing circle'. I thought, 'This is it. This is what I've been looking for all this time.' I phoned them up and went that week. It was held in a disused tomato-packing shed. They tried to make it cosy with carpets, flowers, candles and relaxed music. It was a very pleasant atmosphere. There were about five or six people there who were 'healers' and about 30 to 50 other people. I then went every Wednesday night for about three years. They would open by saying a prayer to 'Dear Father God/Dear Mother God.' Then there would be 'prayers' for a list of people that would be read out. That was called 'distance' or 'absent healing' for people who were sick. Then you could go and sit on a chair and be prayed over or have hands-on healing from one of the 'healers'.

I then started going to their 'open circle' on 'mediumship' on a Monday night, which involved trying to communicate with dead people. There would only be about six or seven people there and it was held at the same place. We would have a 'guided meditation', for which we would sit on chairs in a circle with our eyes closed and relax. The leader would then get us to imagine we were in a field, and take us through the field up a path to the top of a mountain. Once you were up at the top she would leave you there, and the idea was that you would then get communication from beyond. People would have a 'spirit guide' – often a Red Indian – and would get messages from them. Some people had told me to be careful about my involvement. One of them was a friend who was a Christian, but I thought she was being narrow minded. She said that all healing should be done in the name of Jesus, but I thought all born-again Christians were a bunch of wallies. My parents never knew I went to these meetings, but Mark did and he wasn't bothered.

In 1997 our daughter Lillie was born, and soon afterwards the group split. Unpleasantness was creeping in and I just stopped going. At that time I was bothered about how to bring up William regarding spiritual matters. I used to tell him things about spirits – that they existed and things like that. But then I started to wonder whether it was sensible and correct. I didn't feel I knew enough about Christianity. I used to take him to church every now and then, and he used to say it was so boring and I used to think, 'Yeah, it's dreadful.' I didn't know what to do because there was no point in just forcing him to go to mass if he wasn't going to enjoy it. When we did go to church we went to St Joseph's Catholic Church, one of the three Catholic churches on the island. My Christian friend Mandy had mentioned the Alpha course to me quite a few times, describing it as a basic Christianity course. I would say, 'Well, I'm quite interested but I'm not really ready.'

Then one day I was in the school playground picking

William up and found myself chatting to another member of the church, called Dorien. After that, Dorien often invited me to her church group's socials, but I kept putting her off. But in the summer of 1999 I could put her off no longer and I accepted. I went along and found the people were really nice and I enjoyed the evening. I went again about a month later and then started going to their group every fortnight. We would normally have some supper and then perhaps a discussion about something in the Bible. I enjoyed it. It was very gentle and I felt comfortable. They said they had been talking about doing an Alpha course within the group for a long time. They suggested doing one together on a Thursday night and I said, 'I'm terribly sorry, I'm starting an exercise class on that night.' They then changed it to a Wednesday, but the exercise class also changed to a Wednesday, so I thought, 'Phew, thank goodness for that, I'm not going to have to commit myself.' So I said, 'I'm so sorry, I do feel really embarrassed, but the exercise class has changed to a Wednesday night.'

They replied, 'No worries. We'll just change it back to Thursday.'

Around the same time a new person came into our group and the leader asked her to tell the story of how she became a Christian. It turned out her story was all about how she had been drawn into the occult and ended up nearly suicidal. As she spoke my heart was thudding and I said, 'I've got to say something. I've been doing all the same sort of stuff.' She had been in it a lot deeper than I was.

She said to me, 'Have you seen your spirit guide yet?'

And I said, 'Yeah.'

Then she said, 'Get out now. You're in deep trouble.'

It was that experience which convinced me that I had to

do something. I thought of the Alpha course and that evening said, 'Right, I want to do it.' So I started the Alpha course on the Thursday night. We would meet up, have a meal – I absolutely loved it and I kept them all up until around midnight every time, asking so many questions. At the beginning I was quite hostile but they would just laugh about it. On the third week, we were shown a prayer of repentance through which you could ask God into your life. I came home and thought, 'Oh well, I've got nothing to lose. If it's true something will happen. If it's not true then no problem.' And I prayed the prayer. I was sitting on a chair in the kitchen and I started saying sorry for my sins. At first I felt no different, but then it felt as if a light was shining around inside me into all my dark corners. It was this really strange feeling. It showed me things in my character that I didn't even know I had. For example, I didn't like people who talked behind other people's backs, and the light showed me instances where I had done exactly that. I was so horrified to find out that I was actually exactly like the people that I criticised, and I felt really, really sorry.

From that point everything changed. I said, 'Jesus, you are going to have to help me, as I can't change myself.' And I invited him into my life. When I went back to Alpha the following week I said, 'By the way, I said that prayer last week,' and I explained what happened. I didn't tell Mark though. Initially I didn't go to church, but then I went a couple of times to King's Church. It's what I called happy-clappy. I didn't enjoy the first one. The worship side of it was very strange to me, but it got easier. I carried on going to the group every week and I didn't miss a meeting – I loved it. I've hardly missed a week since then actually. After my experience on the third week, we started praying together as a group and I started to feel I could join in quite happily. I suddenly realised that Christianity was so simple, but I had never understood a word of it. It never occurred to me that Jesus died for me as well as for humanity. I also started reading the Bible, and I think I read Mark's Gospel that summer, and then Acts and the letters and everything. I also found I was praying every day – all the time – about everything. It was spontaneous – I prayed to Jesus about whatever came into my head really. I had never prayed like this before. In fact, I remember that when I was about 12, I prayed 33,000 'Hail Mary's for my grandpa who had died. I would pray about 100 a night. I just thought that was the thing to do.

I finished the Alpha course and then I started going to St Joseph's Catholic Church on a Sunday. When I did so, all of a sudden I understood what was going on and it wasn't boring at all. I had come to know it all off by heart, but I had never understood it. I could actually say all the prayers with feeling and mean them. Before it had all just been by rote. I've been going to St Joseph's every Sunday since. I did another Alpha course, using the videos, in the summer of 2000 at King's Church, because a friend of mine called Catherine wanted to do it. She was brought up in a multi-cultural environment and didn't know very much about Jesus. We set up a morning course and several other women joined us. Catherine became a Christian really quickly and she now goes to King's Church.

I had started to pray in the summer of 2000 that Alpha would be run at St Joseph's, but I thought I might be praying for 20 years. Soon afterwards, there was an invitation in our parish newsletter to attend a meeting regarding Alpha, led by David Payne, from the 'Alpha for Catholics' office.

During the meeting I put my hand up and said, 'I'd just like to say that I have already done two Alpha courses and it has brought me back to mass. I hadn't been for years and I loved it.' The priest came straight over to me afterwards and thanked me for saying that, which brought tears to my eyes as I really thought I had put myself on the line.

We started a course in January 2001 and we had 45 people. It was a tremendous success. We had the Alpha videos and most people came every week. We had two drop out I think. We had a day away for the talks on the Holy Spirit and it was really good. The leader of the group prayed for people who were on the course and quite a few had some very nice experiences. At the end of one of the talks on the Alpha video, Nicky Gumbel [Alpha course speaker] reads out a prayer of commitment from the *Why Jesus?* booklet. When the video ended the course leader said to everyone, 'I'm going to pray that prayer again in case anybody didn't catch it, and if anybody would like to say that in their hearts or aloud, please feel free.' The whole room said it aloud, which was amazing.

The difference between the Holy Spirit and the spirituality that I was into before is that the Holy Spirit is for the benefit of others – with self-development (spiritual growth) a bonus. The other is all about self-development – first maybe with a view to ultimately helping others, but I found that I never got around to helping anybody. The chapter on the New Age in *Searching Issues* by Nicky Gumbel really made an impact on me. It was really accurate and very helpful. It doesn't condemn every New Age practice, but it shows that they can lead on to other things. I don't want to deal with any of that New Age stuff now, but I'm glad I did it, because people are more likely to believe me when I say there is a better way, than if I had no knowledge of the subject. If anyone is reading this who might be involved with any of the things I was involved in, I would say, 'Do an Alpha course.' There are other things that they could do, but Alpha is great because you get an opportunity to explore the spiritual side of things in a very non-condemnatory environment, which is very important.

Jesus meant very little to me before the Alpha course. Academically I knew everything, but it didn't have any reality for me. Now he comes into my mind all the time. I am still searching for more knowledge of him and more of the Holy Spirit.

Christine Woodall has helped on several Alpha courses at St Joseph's. She attends a cell group with King's Church and hosts an interdenominational 'Mothers' Prayers' Group once a week.

'I was convinced I was going to die.'

The story of Claire Cooper

Claire Cooper, of St Albans, was on holiday in Italy when she accepted a man's offer to read her palm. His prophecy was simple: 'You are going to have two children and you are going to die at 32.' She forgot about it until ten years later. By then she was 32 and she had two children. This is her story of what happened:

My parents weren't really Christians although I used to go to Sunday school. As a teenager I just dropped away from it. When I went to secondary school I got mixed up in the wrong crowd and went off the rails a bit, getting involved in occasional smoking, shoplifting, playing truant – that sort of thing. I got a variety of jobs over the next few years. When I was 20 I got a job with a car-part company where my boss was an atheist. He often talked about Christianity because his previous secretary had been a Christian and he'd done some research. His atheism was so convincing that I thought, 'Yeah, I think he's right. I don't think there is a God.'

Soon after that I became engaged to a young man and we got a house. I remember saying to a friend at the time, 'I'm so lucky. I've got a boyfriend, I've got a house, I've got all these friends . . .' It was really weird, but within the space of about a month my boyfriend had finished with me, my mum and dad didn't want me home and all of my friends seemed to fall by the wayside. It was a very lonely time. I rented a little bed-sit and would go to work, go home to this little room and that would be it. That would be my life. I didn't see anybody at weekends. I remember crying out to God in that room saying, 'God, is this what my life is all about?'

In about March 1990 I went with two friends, Sarah and Fay, to see a fortune-teller recommended by a girl at work. I had this macabre interest in, 'Ooh, what does the future hold?' We went to see this lady in her flat in Coventry. We waited in her living room and one by one we went into her bedroom to have our fortunes told. She used tarot cards and sort of dice things. She asked me to sit on her bed and she sat next to me. I remember feeling slightly apprehensive and hoped that she wouldn't tell me any bad news. She got me to split the pack of cards and then she put them on the bed. She said that I was going to meet my husband within five days, five weeks or five months. She said he would be two years older than me and that he wouldn't be from Coventry. She then said I would have two children, a boy and a girl, and that I would miscarry with a third. I remember thinking, 'Well, two children and one miscarriage. That's not too bad.'

The lady told us to write down what she had said when we got home and I did. I kept that piece of paper for several years and looked at it sporadically. Lots of the things came true. Soon after that I went to Italy on holiday with my best friend, Fay. One night about half way through the holiday, we went out with two fellows we met. We went to a coffee bar, and while we were sitting round the table one of them said, 'I can read people's palms.' As he was sitting next to me I gave him my hand. I felt slightly apprehensive. He looked at it for a few seconds and then said, 'You're going to have two children and you're going to die at the age of 32.' That took my breath away. I remember feeling a panic, but then I rationalised it and thought, 'Well, I'm only 23. It's miles away.'

After the holiday I got an extra job as a waitress in a restaurant. One day we were working in the kitchens, and one of the chefs and another waitress were talking and joking about palm reading. I joined in and said, 'Can you read palms? Have a look at mine,' and I held out my hand. They looked at my hand and then looked at me with wide eyes and drew their breath. Then they started laughing. Although they probably didn't really see anything, the look in their faces brought back the panic and fear and I thought, 'Maybe that guy in Italy was right.' One of the other waitresses came up to me later and said, 'I can read palms, let me have a look.' I told her about the fortune-teller and the man in Italy. She then looked at my hand and tried to dismiss everything they had said. I knew she was just trying to comfort me, and I was simply left with an even stronger feeling that they had been right.

In about August 1990 I went away again with Fay and two other friends to Corfu. That is when I met my husband Peter. At the time he was working in sales for SmithKline Beecham and lived in St Albans. As Peter wasn't from Coventry and I'd met him within five months of seeing the fortune-teller, I started thinking that perhaps the things she'd said were coming true. Our relationship really developed and after about two years I moved to St Albans to live with him. I had just turned 25. We lived in a bungalow together for the first year and during that year we got engaged. Life was just one round of socialising and I got a good office job. During this time I had no real experience of Christianity.

In 1994 Peter and I got married, and about a couple of months after we were married we found out that I was pregnant with Nathan. I found Nathan's name in the Bible. Peter's mum had one, and whenever we went to their house I would look in it for suitable children's names. Obviously I would read certain passages but it never made any sense. It was gobbledegook. In March 1997 our second son, Samuel, was born. Again I looked through the Bible for his name. We got both the boys baptised. I don't know why really. I think because Peter's family was Catholic and I just went along with this Catholic tradition.

We booked a holiday to Majorca in the May of that year and that was when I turned 30. On that holiday I remember thinking, 'Oh gosh, I'm nearly 32.' I realised that most of the things I'd been told about my future had come true, and I started to think, 'Am I going to die now?' From that point on I lived in fear. At around the same time I started getting fixated with wanting another baby. Peter was very reluctant but I kept going on and on at him. In the end he said, 'If you want one we'll have one.' I got pregnant in July 1999 and by then I had actually turned 32 and I started thinking, 'Oh no, am I going to die in childbirth?' I would always be looking at myself and thinking, 'Have I got any lumps or any moles?' It was totally irrational. I would think about my death daily and my heart would really accelerate and I would get panicky about it. I would put it to the back of my mind and then it would re-surface. I told Peter about my feelings but there wasn't really anything he could do. I was convinced I was going to die.

About eight or nine weeks into the pregnancy I had a

miscarriage and after that I thought, 'Oh gosh, I've had the miscarriage. I really am going to die now.' That Christmas we planned a holiday to Portugal to have a break. I was petrified of going. I thought, 'If I'm going to die and it's in an aeroplane I will take everyone with me.' I was so worried that I would be killing my boys. However we went on the holiday and came back safely. It was January 2000 and I was due to turn 33 in the May. I thought I had months to live. Two weeks before my birthday I had a panic attack in the middle of the night and I couldn't breathe. I thought, 'This is it, I'm having a heart attack.' I woke Peter up and said, 'I'm dying. I'm dying. I can't breathe.' He didn't know what to say at first, then he was telling me to take it easy and breathe. One minute I would be really hot and the next shivering cold. It was just a case of trying to breathe normally. Once I calmed down a bit it did go back to normal. The next morning Peter said, 'I think you ought to go to the doctor.'

That day I went to the doctor and she was fantastic. I told her everything that was going on. She said, 'Well, you obviously think you've only got two weeks to live, which is why you're having this panic attack.' She wanted to see me the following week and then after my birthday. I saw her the following week and I was actually a bit better because I had unloaded everything on to this woman. I then saw her after my birthday and I was fine because I had got through my birthday. I was like, 'I haven't died.' From then on I started reading self-help books about anxiety and depression and started getting myself sorted out.

Nathan started school and in September that year I started a part-time job at Safeway. One day I was at the school and I noticed an Alpha poster in the poster case at the school gate. It just said something like, 'What is the meaning of life?' I thought, 'I want to know that.' I'd been through what felt like hell and I'd reached that point where I wanted to know what it was all about. There was a name at the bottom of the poster, 'Carol Jacobs'. I knew this lady so when I next saw her I said, 'What's this Alpha all about?'

She said, 'It's a very up-to-date Christianity course.'

I remember thinking, 'Oh.' It wasn't really what I was expecting to hear. I think I thought it would be a sort of psychology course or something like that. Carol told me there would be a meal followed by a video and a chat. I must admit the meal part attracted me. I thought, 'Oh, that sounds nice.' I quite liked the social side of it too. I would get quite bored in the evenings because Peter would often get home late from work. I couldn't find a babysitter for the first week, which made me even more determined to go on it.

I went along to the second week of the course. It was held at Christchurch in St Albans, which is a very modern church. I went by myself and I was a bit nervous, but Carol met me at the door and really looked after me. There was another lady there that I knew. She had missed the first week as well so we started together, which was really nice. We had the meal and then watched the video in a different room, followed by the chat. It was all very informal. The following week I was working at Safeway. It was the Thursday morning. I was sitting on the floor next to the shampoos thinking, 'Shall I go to Alpha tonight?' At that moment a lady reached down to pick up a shampoo bottle. It was Carol. She said, 'Oh, how did you find it last week?'

I said, 'Oh, I don't know – but I'll see the course out.'

That night there was something in the talk that made me interested. I then started to really love the videos and was just drinking it all in. We got into the third or fourth week and the atmosphere was really good. It finished at 10pm and we would be hanging around talking until 11pm. Around the same time my friend Glenda said she had felt the Holy Spirit. I thought, 'Holy Spirit? Well, I'll believe in God if I feel that Holy Spirit. I won't believe it otherwise.' Soon afterwards I woke up in the middle of the night and felt the Holy Spirit. I felt this wonderful sensation. I can't explain it. My whole body had this tingling sensation and I couldn't believe it. It must have been about midnight. I had just woken up and it was just there. I absolutely knew it was God. I then fell asleep and was woken up again a few hours later and experienced the same thing for about an hour. I just lay there experiencing it and it was just wonderful. I just remember thinking, 'There is a God. There is a God.' It just bowled me over. That was Friday, November 3. In the morning I said to Peter, 'I felt the Holy Spirit last night – I really did.'

He was like, 'Yeah, yeah.'

I then bought myself a Bible from a shop in St Albans. Later when I sat reading it, it made sense for the first time. At this point I was interested in finding a church to go to. I said to Peter, 'I want to go to Holy Trinity Brompton.' We went to a communion service and after taking communion, I sat back down and they started singing that song, 'Amazing Grace'. The lines, 'I once was lost but now am found' seemed to be repeated quite a lot. Then I realised that I had been baptised as a baby on November 5, 1967 – the year I was born. Now here I was taking communion on November 5, 2000 – exactly 33 years later. I was reborn. When I realised that, I just cried and cried and cried, and this song was going on and on and I just carried on crying. I was so overwhelmed. Since then things have gone from strength to strength.

I finished Alpha at Christmas and after that I was really keen for Peter to do the course. About a week or so later Peter had a bad dream about work – he had been having a tough time – and he thought, 'Well, I really don't want this problem to keep going on at work. I'll give Alpha a go and see if God can help me.' That was a turning point for him. He went on the next Alpha course and has since become a Christian.

After going on the Alpha course Jesus became such a big thing for me. All my life I have been blind to it and all of a sudden I can see. My friend across the road recently told me that I have changed. She said I'm more peaceful. That's true. I don't have fear any more. Occasionally I will have a little tiny blip and I just pray and I'm back to normal again. Jesus has healed me. He's making me the person I'm meant to be. I go to church at Christchurch now, where I did Alpha. I love it. I'm also helping out on an Alpha course now, which is fun.

Now I have utter contempt towards palm reading and fortune-telling and that sort of thing. There is something in the Bible that talks about God's peace that transcends all understanding. That is truly what I feel and it can't come from anywhere else.

Peter and Claire Cooper's third child – Grace Elizabeth – was born on 6th January 2002. 'Jesus is a big part of my life' says Claire. 'I have a much deeper and closer relationship with him now.'

3

'I don't do tears, but I cried my eyes out.'

The story of Tony Bolt

Painter and decorator Tony Bolt of Battersea, south London, was close to separating from his live-in girlfriend, Ronnie, when he came on the Alpha course in the summer of 2000. As part of the group being filmed by ITV for their forthcoming documentary series, he did not reveal the extent of the issues he was facing. But the course was to have an extraordinary impact, not only on his own life, but also on the lives of his girlfriend and their five-year-old son, Josh. Here he tells the full story:

I was born in Lambeth and was brought up in Putney with my parents. I have three brothers. No one in our family went to church. We did Sunday school once, but it wasn't for us. At 15 I got a job with a builder, did a full apprenticeship and did very well. I'd hated school, but I really enjoyed college. I went to work for a firm called Ashby and Horners and had a great time. We did Buckingham Palace, Kensington Palace . . . wonderful places. In Buckingham Palace, you have 12 weeks over the summer period when they are all at Balmoral. After a while, I went self-employed and the business went up and down. I wasn't doing it right – ducking and diving, working for cash when I could. I was buying dodgy stuff – cheap, hookey, back-of-a-lorry stuff. Eventually I had a choice of going bankrupt or doing something called an IVA – Independent Voluntary Arrangement – which meant I would pay back creditors over a course of so many years. My mum re-mortgaged the house and for ten years I was paying back nearly £1,000 a month. It's not been easy.

I was into pubbing and clubbing – heavy drinking and drugs as well. I did cocaine for about three or four years. Every weekend I would get my gear and that would be it. I met Ronnie in 1996. Although I gave up the drugs (apart from when friends were around and I'd have a line with them), the heavy drinking continued. I had always drunk. Thursday, Friday, Saturday and Sunday it was a case of 'drink till you're drunk.' I would be blottoed after ten pints of lager.

I met Ronnie when she was a barmaid in my local pub, the Maltese Cat, in Roehampton. We started going out and a year later, in October 1996, she told me she was pregnant. It was a shock. Ronnie was 23 and had just moved down from Middlesbrough. She had got her life settled and did not want children. We both thought about abortion, but I just said to her, 'I'll support you – but you have got to carry the child so it is up to you.' So we ummed and arred for the 12 weeks that you've got, and eventually she said, 'We'll keep it.' I was pleased. I gave her a big bunch of flowers. We were living together then in this tiny little studio flat in Putney. I asked her to marry me in December. I still didn't believe in marriage, but thought it was the decent thing to do. Josh was born on July 25, 1997.

At first Ronnie was very happy, but afterwards she got quite depressed. We went through quite a lot that first year. I was working all this time – paying back bills and debts. We were paying back so much money that we didn't have enough money to live. So I started doing Karaoke nights. We borrowed £1,000 and we got this little PA system, a CD player and some Karaoke discs and started doing pubs and clubs. I found I could earn cash really quickly and pay the bills and have some money for ourselves. It helped, but our relationship was suffering because I was so tired. I was working day and night, five nights a week. I didn't know what day of the week it was. With the Karaoke, it would be 1 or 2am by the time I got home – and I would be up at 6am again to go to work. It wasn't any good for our relationship. We were arguing so much that it got to the stage that I would go to the pub before going home to have a few pints to relax. It was terrible.

As well as this, we had a bad time with our accommodation. We were put in council bed and breakfast at one stage; then we lived with my mum – which was really strained; and then we went to temporary accommodation in Battersea – a kind of prefab where you share the bathroom and toilets. In March 1999 we were offered a beautiful little council flat in Battersea. It was a two bedroom flat and we did it up.

In November 1999, I did a Karaoke night for the family of a friend. I knew the family well. Usually it would have been a night of glorified drink – whisky, cider – heavy. We would all have got slaughtered. But the difference was amazing. The drink was cans of lager, lemonade, tea and coffee. And they were so full of love, so happy. It turned out they had become Christians a couple of years before. I went along to their church a few times on a Sunday. As we came up to Christmas, I said to Ronnie, 'We'll see Christmas through and then in the New Year, I am moving back to my mum's.' We split up, but I came back after a week. It was all too much for me, even though we couldn't get on. I couldn't bear not to see Josh, our son. I just couldn't do it.

Then a friend of mine from work, John Falzon, mentioned his church, Holy Trinity Brompton. He said, 'Come along.' So I went to a 5pm service and at the end we were all standing up and Sandy Millar, the vicar, said, 'Now I want everyone to sit down – apart from people who feel they are searching for something. Please stay standing and keep your eyes closed.' He said a prayer and at the end he looked straight at me and said, 'We are going to give you a *Why Jesus?* book and an invitation to Alpha as you leave. Please come.'

I did the Alpha course in summer 2000. My friend John mentioned to me that they were going to be doing a TV documentary on the Alpha course, and would I be interested in being filmed for it. I said, 'No.' Later I had a telephone call from the TV people and went to meet them. They asked me if I'd be in the group of ten being filmed. Ronnie went mad about me being involved with Christians. Her friends had told her they took people's money and lured them away from their families. I said to her, 'Well, I'm skint anyway – and we don't get on, so I'll be fine.' Ronnie didn't like me being on TV either. We were still living together, but it was terrible. I made life much worse for us than it should have been. Every time she moaned, I would say, 'Right . . .' and I would walk out and go down the pub. That would be it. I used to think, 'If I'm not there, then we can't row.' But it just made things worse when I got back, because she would stop talking to me. So we didn't talk.

So I started this Alpha course. I couldn't talk about all that was going on with Ronnie in front of the television cameras. It was too private. But after the group sessions, we would all go down to the pub, and there I talked about it to Meno, Minnie, Gillian – to several of them. That's where we really spoke. Me and Meno have got a lot in common. He had been through similar stuff to me and that's why we relate so much to each other.

By four weeks into the course, I felt as if I was changing in myself and things were beginning to make sense. One night I sat Ronnie down and said, 'What's wrong?' I looked straight into her eyes and said, 'Tell me what's wrong. What don't you like about me?' At that point she got it all off her chest.

She said, 'You're just drinking . . . you're always going out and you're doing stuff. You're always working. You never think about us.'

At the end I said, 'Well, I'll try.' That's what changed a lot for us in our relationship.

Amanda Cowley [who led the group with her husband, Paul] gave me *The Message* translation of the New Testament, and I started reading about Jesus in Mark's Gospel. Ronnie was invited to come to the weekend but in the end she didn't and I took Josh. It was fine because by that time we were talking much more. She went to a party. It was all a bit tiring for those of us in the TV group, because we had a lot of interviews to do while everyone else was just enjoying themselves. That evening Nicky [Nicky Gumbel, the Alpha course speaker] invited the Holy Spirit to come. I just stood there and soon afterwards he came over to me and said, 'Would you like me to pray for you?'

I said, 'Yes please.'

He said, 'Close your eyes,' and as he prayed all I can say is that I just felt so safe, as if God was saying, 'I've got you and I'll never let you go.' Soon after that my legs just went and I fell – wallop – crash on the floor. I fell into Minnie behind me.

I said sorry to God for all the drugs, the relationships I've had, living with Ronnie and not getting on – personal stuff. After what seemed like an hour I got up and I can honestly say that it was that day I became a Christian, and Jesus is in my life now. I felt so forgiven and, well, the love just poured out. The others thought I had gone mad. I got back and told Ronnie about this experience. I gave her a big cuddle and said to her, 'I really love you. I've always loved you. I didn't realise.'

Then towards the end of the course, she went, 'I'm going to go on this Alpha course.' She came to the supper at the end of my course and then went on the next one. I was helping on that course, but I asked if we could be in different groups so she could do her own journey. She was in Jonathan and Isabelle Gill's group and it was the same story – she made great friends and had a great time. She had an experience and gave her life to the Lord as well. She has a Catholic background and so she has been going to her local Catholic church since then. Josh and I go too – and to Holy Trinity as well. We've changed. Relationship-wise, if there's a problem, we sort it out. We never leave anything any more.

If there is something she doesn't like me doing, then she tells me or, if not, then I'll know there is something wrong because she goes quiet. It is a question of communication.

After Christmas 2000, I picked her up from work. We were in the van and I said, 'There's something I need to tell you when we get home.'

She said, 'What is it?'

I said, 'Nothing bad. Don't worry. I've got to tell you when we get home.' Then I said, 'Oh, I can't wait.' I pulled the van over and said, 'Do you love me?'

She said, 'Of course I love you.'

And I said, 'And I love you.' Then I said, 'Do you want to spend the rest of your life with me?' And the tears . . .

She said, 'What are you saying?'

I went, 'We should be married. Shall we get married?'

She said, 'Yes,' sobbing. And that was it.

We asked Nicky Gumbel to marry us, never dreaming he would say yes, but he did. He spent so much of his time sitting with us. We went around to his house to work out the marriage service. We felt guided by God throughout it all. Friends of ours told us about this fantastic cake-maker and the wedding cake was wonderful. It was such a blessing. And all the time I was praying that God would fill the place, that the Spirit of God would be in the church (which I knew it would be but even more so). We invited 250 friends and family – most of whom never go to church. It was 11 August 2001. We invited Ronnie's priest to come along and Nicky said, 'Well, why doesn't he do part of the service? Why can't he do the blessings and the prayers?' So he did. Paul did a reading for us, Amanda made a special prayer up personally for us. Ronnie's family all came down from

Middlesbrough. It must have cost them a fortune, but they wanted to be there for that day.

At the rehearsal the night before, Nicky had said, 'You stand at the front, your best man there . . .' and he saw me planning to look round at once. He said, 'No Tony. If you want to look around, I'll give you the nod when she comes through the doors, and you turn around and there you are. That will work perfectly.'

He didn't tell me how lovely she'd look. When the day came, he gave me the signal to look around and I spun around and I just . . . the way she looked . . . I can never ever forget . . . She was absolutely beautiful. She is beautiful anyway, but she was stunning – the dress, the flowers, her hair, her make up, her nails. I just cried. I couldn't help it. I don't do tears, but I cried my eyes out. My brother had to get hold of my arm and I was just a blubbering mess by the time she got there. We walked up the steps to Nicky, which seemed like a mile away, and I am going, 'You look beautiful.' We were walking up the stairs and Nicky's eyes were filling up as well – and Ronnie's were too. We started saying our vows and Ronnie couldn't speak, she was so emotional. So I took a tissue out of my pocket and gave it to her and said, 'You're all right now.' I'd got myself together and calmed myself down, and then the service went so fast. Then we were married. Nicky said, 'I now pronounce you husband and wife. You may kiss the bride . . .' and the place erupted. Everyone clapped and cheered. Nicky made the service. The address he gave was so personal because we know him.

Everybody was blown away by the service. It was the best day of my life. It was the best. We did the speeches and what Ronnie didn't know was that I had planned a holiday for us. The passports hadn't been easy because Josh needed a passport for himself. I tried to put him on my passport but you can't do that anymore. Anyway, I managed to tell Ronnie he needed one some time in the future, so I got it. What she didn't know was that I had been giving my mum some money to put away. I booked a holiday to Gran Canaria and I got Josh's passport after queuing up in Petty France all day. During the wedding speeches I thanked everybody and said the normal stuff. Then I said, 'By the way, I've got a special gift for Ronnie.' I had this shoe box with all padding in and the flight tickets at the bottom. So at the end of the speech, I got this box out and said, 'I've got a little present for you darling.' She looked at me and I said, 'Open it.'

She was shaking as she opened it and then she saw the tickets for the two of us. She burst into tears again and said, 'What? Just me and you?'

And I said, 'Open up the rest.' She pulled the bottom of the box back and there was Josh's passport at the bottom. It worked so well. And everybody started crying again.

My family are still saying when they ring up, 'That wedding was the best wedding we have ever been to.'

We were in Gran Canaria for two weeks. It was the best time. I was reading the Bible and we were talking about Jesus – especially with Josh. Josh is amazing. I was telling him about Jesus' miracles, and one day we read about how he had healed the man who had been a cripple from birth. The next day we were walking down the beach and there was a man with one leg. Normally kids would just point and stare, but Josh said, 'Daddy, see that man? Would Jesus heal him?'

I said, 'Of course he would, darling . . . We like Jesus,

don't we?' And that's how he has been. It builds your faith up more. They are so innocent and they only know the truth, don't they? The truth is Jesus.

We pray every night – me and Ronnie. We pray with Josh but he goes to bed about 7.30pm. In the evenings I pray – by myself and with Ronnie. Lola [another of the ITV group of ten] and I now lead a home group.

Two years ago if we'd had Christians knocking at the door, I wouldn't have answered the door to them. I'd have just thought they were a mad bunch, not on my wavelength. I wouldn't go anywhere near them. You get this stereotyped Christian – the sandals, the beard and the guitar, and being happy all the time – but it's not like that. It is real – a living relationship with God. People used to tell me – even when I went to this East London church – about this relationship with God and I thought, 'What are you talking about? A relationship with God?'

My mum had brought us up to pray because of what my dad used to do. Dad would come back from his drinking and be violent. Mum used to say every Sunday afternoon, 'Let's pray that daddy's going to be all right and not cause any problems.' That's where the prayers came from back then. So I always believed in God, but as for a 'relationship' and 'being a Christian' – no way. Two years ago I thought Jesus was one of these disciples that you hear about, who spreads the Word of God. I didn't know anything about him. To me, he was not the Son of God – certainly not. Now I think he is wonderful. I would say that Jesus is our Saviour. He came here just for us, to forgive us for our sins, and we can have a relationship with him. To me, he is my best mate.

My business had been doing so badly, but I prayed to God that the business would be blessed. I said to God, 'I'll do anything you want, but if you want me to carry on with this business, show me where I am going wrong.' The first thing I did was to start paying tax. I have never paid so much tax in my life, which is great. I have got eight staff now, who are all on PAYE. I only had sub-contractors before. Now it is all perfectly legal and above board, which is killing me, because it is so much paperwork. I used to get letters from the National Insurance saying, 'You owe six years. When are you going to pay some?' I am up-to-date now. Jesus has done that for me. It is so much better, because I haven't got those worries anymore. Every morning before I go to work, I pray that he will look after me and my family, and that he'll be around my driving, the work I do, the jobs I go to.

As for Ronnie and me, our relationship was going nowhere. There's no way we would have been married. I probably would have ended up hurting her or, at best, just moving out. She probably would have gone back to her family in Middlesbrough. I love Ronnie. I really love her and she loves me – I know that. I tell her I love her every day.

Tony and Ronnie Bolt continue to attend Holy Trinity Brompton where they have also attended The Marriage Course. Tony says: 'Jesus is at the centre of our lives.'

'I went to Alpha to disprove God. I thought,
". . . I can argue with the best of them." '

The story of Ian Morris

*Rugby-playing Ian Morris had no interest in Chris-
tianity when his wife went on an Alpha course and
declared that she was going to start attending church.
Later, she suggested that he too go on an Alpha
course. After some thought he agreed, on the condition that she would not complain if he put everyone
else off their faith because of his arguments. This is
what happened . . .*

My childhood was happy, but also pretty tough. My dad,
a printer and union man, was 47 when I was born and
was made unemployed when I was just ten. He never got
another job. It was a tragedy for him. He was a very intelli-
gent man but slightly stubborn and very confident in his own
decisions. In later life I know he looked back at some of the
decisions he made and regretted what he had done with his
life. He had opportunities to go places with work, but never
took them up because he was so committed to the trade
union and wanted to remain one of the guys on the shop
floor.

Mum and dad weren't religious at all. Dad was anti and
mum, although she had gone to church until she was about

14 or 15, chose not to carry on with it. I went to an awful school which later closed down, because out of a year of 240 people they had only two pupils pass O-level maths and five pass O-level English. It really was appalling. I was considered one of the brighter kids and was always thought of as a bit of a swot, but I also had a tendency to get in a number of fights for varying reasons. I had this combination of being quite bright but also with a bit of a flash temper.

Later I went to college where I did a lot of partying, but managed to get A-levels in Chemistry and Biology. I then got a job with a pharmaceutical manufacturer called Cyanamid – first as a microbiology lab technician and then as a chemist. I always had this temper which could go off at any point. I used to play Sunday league football and had what they called a 'suspect disciplinary record', where I got a number of red cards and sendings off for punching people and generally being a nuisance. My quite sharp wit meant I could also be very unkind. I could take the micky out of people and be really quite unkind to them, but didn't really bat an eyelid about it.

I worked very hard. Money was what I was really after. Although my salary wasn't huge, I was working virtually every Saturday and Sunday, doing a lot of overtime. All the money I earned, though, I then spent on going out on the beer Friday, Saturday and Sunday nights. I never had enough money and between the ages of 18 and 21 I ran up about a £4,500 credit card bill – most of it drinking related. I stopped playing Sunday league football when I got a one-year ban for three red cards in three successive weeks. I wasn't really bothered, though, and decided to play rugby, which I considered open, honest and fair aggression, whereas football was niggly. I was always probably a couple of stone over what I should have been, so I tended to play second, third, fourth team rugby for Gosport and Fareham RFC. Around these rugby teams there was a colossal drinking culture and, being a bit of a character, everyone soon knew who I was. I was drinking a colossal amount – probably 35 to 40 pints over the course of a Thursday, Friday, Saturday, Sunday. On Thursday I would have five, Friday I'd have ten, Saturday it would be 15, and then Sunday would be five again. It was a large amount but then I was a big guy, and if you drink that much, OK you still get drunk, but the five pints is the same as only having one or two for normal people. It was just what I did.

At work I had a bad attitude and I was one of those people who would rail against authority, and if something wasn't right, then I would stand up in a meeting and bang the table and say, 'It's not right.' I probably got myself labelled as a bit of a trouble-maker and it was probably a pretty fair label. If somebody earned five pounds a year more than I did, then I resented them for it. It became a kind of burning thing in me. I would do all the overtime, earn all the money, but it never got me anywhere because as soon as I got it, I spent it and then spent some more.

While in the lab I was in a number of relationships with people I worked with. Then something happened to me which changed things. I began to have problems with my eyesight and starting knocking over flasks and things in the lab. I had my eyes tested and it was discovered that I had a genetic condition called 'retonitis pigmentosa' – which effectively meant I was growing progressively partially sighted. There was a narrowing in my field of vision which was particularly pronounced at night, when I was soon almost completely blind. When my bosses at work found out, it was a question of, 'Well, we're not sure we really want you working in the lab with buckets of dangerous chemicals.' So eventually they gave me a new role out of the lab environment and into an office, working as part of the planning team.

While I had been working in the lab, a girl called Nicky had been working in the lab next door to me and we had hated each other. She was a bit hyper and tense, and with my ascerbic wit, I used to have great fun in pulling her tail and winding her up and then watching her go off. Then, a little later, we met again at a work social evening. We had a bit of a dance and I thought, 'Well, she's not that bad.' Walking home with a mutual friend called Steve, I said, 'I think she's quite all right. Look, I'm off on holiday for the next week and a half. Can you test the water very cautiously and let me know the score when I come back?' Steve (the blunt guy that he is) took the 'My mate fancies you' approach, and she said, 'I wonder who that is?'

She had just come out of this long relationship that she had been in for about six and a half years, and had had a lot of hurt in the break up. However she thought, 'Well, OK', and we started to go out. I was 23 and Nicky was 22. We just hit it off straight away – this was in July/August 1992 – and we've been together ever since. I moved out of my parents' home and in with her, and then we bought our first house together in the early part of 1995 and got married in the May. Our relationship was a very fiery one from the start. I think Nicky was carrying quite a lot of hurt from her previous relationship and we rowed an awful lot. There were parts of our relationship where we didn't actually like bits of each other very much, but we kind of glossed over those bits and focussed on the bits that we had in common. I was very self-motivated and was still determined to earn a lot of money. Nicky had a good job and I was moving on well, so I felt we were going places.

To me, people who went to church were sad people who needed a crutch in their life because they weren't reliant on themselves. My life was full of working, drinking, going out, doing things, living it up. I wouldn't say it was hedonistic, but it was very materialistic. In 1995, Nicky got promoted and that was great. But then in February 1996, she started getting terrible panic attacks and the wheels came off the bus. I didn't understand depression and mental illness, and I didn't want to understand them and I didn't want them to be happening to Nicky. Basically she said, 'I can't go on' and my first thought was, 'Oh no. I don't need this.' She was then off work for quite a while and went on anti-depressants to wind her down. I think for the first two weeks she just slept. After that she began to get a bit better, which was great.

Then one day she suddenly said, 'Oh, I've bought a Bible and I'm going to go to church.'

And I said something like, 'Ah, great! I'm so pleased.'

She said, 'Oh, I thought you would be angry.'

I said, 'Oh, no, no, no. If that's what you want to do, love, then that's great.'

I was very much in love with her and it hurt me to see her like she had been. Anything that I considered would help her get back together I was fine with. It fitted my idea of the church perfectly. She was struggling with the things of life and here was religion as a crutch to get her through it. So I said, 'You go do it, girl, because if that does you good then that's fine.' I thought, 'Well actually, it's not such a bad thing, because each Sunday she'll be off to church, and I'll get a lie in and potter about and get myself something to eat and that will be great.' I wasn't drinking so much by this stage. It had kind of backed off, but if I went out with one of the guys we would still have 8, 10, 12 pints.

So Nicky was off going to church and loving it, and then one day in September she said to me, 'Why don't you come on an Alpha course?'

I said, 'What do you mean "come on an Alpha course"?'

She said, 'Well, it's a chance to come and discuss Christianity.'

I said, 'Whoah, no, that's not a good idea.'

She said, 'Why not?'

I said, 'Well you've got to look at it this way. I am red hot at arguing with people – do you agree?'

'Yes.'

'Well, frankly you're going to wheel up a load of mimsy Christians who are going to try and convince me that they're right – and I am going to blast them and you won't like that, so I am not going.'

She said, 'No, no, no, I won't mind.'

I said, 'Look, OK, I'll go on one condition – that you don't get stroppy with me when I win the argument and people don't turn up on Sunday because I have convinced them that God doesn't exist.'

And she was like, 'Yep, come along.'

And I said, 'Right, you reckon your lads are up to taking me on – then I'm going to go for it.' So I went along to disprove God. I thought, 'If we're going to have a ruck about this, that's fine because I can argue with the best of them.'

I went along and it was a kind of church I hadn't seen before. It wasn't a great tall building, with a high vaulted roof and a spire and gold bits, and what you would expect a church to be. No, this church – called 'Logos' – was based in a fairly unsightly hut in the middle of a housing estate. So I thought, 'Right, OK.' Then I went in and started talking to people. Although some of them fitted my 'Christian' stereotype, there were lots of others who made me think, 'Hmmm, you don't make sense because you're a bit real to be a Christian. You've actually got some rough edges about you.' They would talk about Jesus in a way which was relevant. I also felt kind of inhibited as far as my natural aggression was concerned. It never usually bothered me to go in and tear people up. If people wanted an argument, they would get one – and if they burst into tears, well sorry, that was their look out. But for some reason at Alpha I didn't feel like I could do that. It was strange.

The social context was very different to what I was used to. It was having a meal and a pleasant chat, rather than drinking ten pints and singing rowdy songs or having a crude joke with your mates. But I enjoyed it. All of these people were nice people and they were genuine. I had never come across that before. I didn't mix in circles where there were nice people. I thought people were out for themselves. I had a lot of acquaintances – I could walk down the high street on a Saturday morning and I would bump into at least half a dozen people that I knew – but I couldn't say that I had many really close friends. Yet these people on Alpha sort of accepted me as I was and were friendly towards me, and I enjoyed that. I felt, 'This is really quite touching.' I thought, 'Yeah, this is what has been so good for Nicky.' She had completely changed – a complete transformation. We used to be quite spiky with each other, but now we weren't having so many arguments as she was always looking to make peace. I was quite happy to go along with that. She had a much more positive outlook on life, and there was a care and an interest in other people that she hadn't had before, which made me think, 'Wow'. The panic attacks still occurred, but not as frequently.

The Alpha Day Away was held on a Saturday when I was already doing something and I thought, 'Oh no, I can't believe this! Why is it on this Saturday?' My best friend, David, had said to me, 'Ian, on Saturday 4th, Gosport are playing Portsmouth at home. It's an early kick off and then it's England versus Ireland in the afternoon, so we'll go and watch the game down at the park then come back to my house, have a few beers and watch the international.'

'Superb', I'd said. Then I found out that was the Alpha Day Away.

I mentioned it to Nicky and she said, 'Well, you did say you'd do the whole course.'

I said, 'Yes, but . . .'

She said, 'Well, it's up to you.'

I then thought, 'Well, I suppose I can tape the rugby and watch it in the evening.' So in the end I cancelled my arrangements with Dave and decided to go to the Alpha day.

I wasn't particularly worried about it – I just saw it as another part of the course. I got there and we did the talk sessions, and then in the afternoon they said they were going to start praying for people. I was still pretty cynical but liked the people and enjoyed spending time with them. They were a good bunch. There was a little bit of space at the front where they were praying for someone, so I thought, 'Well, I'd better join in – at least so I can be seen to be playing the part.' I closed my eyes and put my hands together and thought, 'Well, that's what people do when they pray.'

Then the pastor, Richard, made an announcement. He said, 'We are about to start praying for Stuart (another guest on the course), and if anybody has a picture that can encourage him, would they like to share it?' Suddenly, I got this vivid picture in my mind. It was literally like a television coming on. My mouth went dry because I have never been imaginative or creative or that kind of thing. The picture was of a desert and there was this small tree in the sand. The winds were blowing from all directions and bouncing it about, but its roots were set firm. I thought, 'I don't like this' but I felt compelled to speak out what I'd seen.

After that, I felt a little queasy and so I decided, 'I'm going to get some fresh air.' I walked out of the church and stood there breathing deeply.

A guy was there doing some maintenance and he said, 'Are you all right?'

I said, 'I've just come over a bit strange.'

He said, 'Yeah, it happens like that sometimes, but you don't want to miss out.'

I said, 'I suppose not.' So I turned round and went back in again.

Later, they asked if they could pray for me and I said, 'Yeah, OK.' So I sat on this plastic chair and a group gathered around me, laid their hands on me and started to pray for me. Richard, the pastor, said to me, 'I feel God saying, "What do you want?" '

I thought, 'Well OK, God. If you're real, you prove it.' I'm not a person given to emotion but I suddenly felt this terrible darkness. It was like all the bad things I'd done and all the unkind things I'd said . . . At that, I just broke down and sobbed and sobbed and sobbed in this rickety hut, surrounded by these people who basically I'd only just got acquainted with. I couldn't stop crying and I sobbed uncontrollably. They continued to pray for me and suddenly there was this change. It was like a switch thrown inside me and then this weight lifted off me, and I felt this real elation. It was like every nerve in my body was alive. I just felt God saying, 'This is me and this is what I've got for you.' And I had this sense that God really was real and could change in a second the way that your life is.

Suddenly all the rest of the Alpha course made sense – all the stuff about redemption and your sins being wiped clean. As far as I was concerned that was it. And there and then I said a prayer asking God for the forgiveness of all the sins I'd done in my life, and inviting Jesus in to be Lord of my life, and to guide me and show me the way that I should be going. There was this knowledge that everything that I had been chasing up to that moment was meaningless. It was as if God opened my eyes. I thought, 'What a waste I've made of my life.'

I completed the Alpha course and then did it again as a helper. After that, my whole approach to people really changed. All my anger and resentment had gone. The second Alpha course was probably more enjoyable than the first, because I had that passion for God within me and I really wanted to learn. Nicky was obviously elated and we threw ourselves into church life quite deeply. We got involved in a house group and never missed a Sunday. In August 1997, I was baptised in Stokes Bay in the Solent, which was absolutely fantastic. We've got a baptismal pool in the church but it's only 6ft long, and I am 6ft 4, so I figured they would take the top of my head off like a boiled egg. I asked if it would be possible to be baptised outside. The whole thing kind of snowballed and we ended up having a fantastic day, with several other local churches and a local Christian band on a sunny Sunday afternoon – and they baptised me which was great.

When I had become a Christian I gave all my career desires and ambitions over to God, and by his grace everything has been taken care of. I moved companies and joined a credit card manufacturer called Gem Plus. I had set out goals that I wanted to achieve in my life, and I just gave them to God saying that they didn't matter – whatever he wanted for my life was right. One of my original goals was to be a manager by the time I was 30, and I got the title Logistics Manager at 28. God keeps opening things up for me. I then got a role as UK Purchasing Manager, which was fantastic. In 1998, we started leading a house group. We sometimes had sixteen people crammed into our living room and it was wonderful. I was also speaking on Alpha.

Then at the end of 1999, the world kind of fell apart for us. We had been waiting and waiting and praying for a family for nearly two and a half years, and finally Nicky became pregnant. We really praised God. Then, tragically, she miscarried at six weeks, which for us was absolutely devastating. It shook our faith to the very foundations. My understanding and experience of God was that he was going to look after us and make sure nothing terrible was going to happen to us – but it didn't work out like that. In our grief, we basically fell apart. We gave up running the house group and effectively gave up going to church for a few weeks.

Then, about a month later, when we were still in a very bad way, Nicky dropped her Bible down the stairs by mistake. As she stooped to pick it up, she saw that it had fallen open at a particular page. She read it and it said something along the lines of, 'Things aren't the way they appear on the outside.' That was a Friday. Then, the next day, we got a letter from one of the guys who had been in our house group but had moved away to college. He was a young lad who was very quiet and slightly insecure, but he sent us a letter saying that God had moved him to pray all night for us recently. He said he felt God was saying, 'Prepare to be amazed.' We looked at it and just thought, 'Yeah' in a negative way. Then, on the Sunday, we did a pregnancy test and it was positive. We then had probably nine of the most intense months we've ever had in our lives, worrying whether it would go wrong or not. Then, on 6 August 2000, Thomas turned up fit and well and he is absolutely perfect. It all means I now have a very different perspective on God. Our experiences have really challenged everything we thought we knew, and we feel that we're now coming out the other side, but differently. I think we had a limited perspective on God.

Jesus has completely changed my personality. For me, life was about what you could achieve for yourself. It was all very much self-centered. Now Jesus has shown me that life is all about him. I've almost certainly got much more peace now than I ever had and our marriage is now so much stronger.

Ian and Nicky Morris and their family now attend Portsmouth Family Church, near their home in Hampshire. Their second child, Noah John, was born in July 2003.

4

'There was deep-rooted hatred between us.'

The story of Len & Yvette Stanley

After 13 years of coping with furious rows and 'deep-rooted hatred' Yvette Stanley and her husband Len were divorced. That was when Len, an outdoor training instructor in the Army, went on Alpha and began a relationship with God which brought the family back together. Here, beginning with Yvette, they tell the story:

Yvette's story

When Len and I got married I thought it was great. I thought, 'This is it.' But it didn't quite turn out as I imagined it would. We had been married for about six months when he went to Denmark for a fortnight on a training exercise. A short time later, he called up and it transpired he had been 'seeing' somebody in Denmark. That's when the rot set in, shall we say. And it just went on. We carried on but I was very disappointed. Part of me wanted to walk away but another part of me thought, 'No, you can't. You've just got married. People have spent all this money giving you presents. You can't then turn around six months later and say, "Sorry".'

I felt a complete failure to think that my husband had gone away with somebody. I thought, 'I must have been doing something wrong, it must be my fault.' Every time he did it, all the way through my married life, I continued to think it was my fault, that it was something I had done. I've never had friends. I wouldn't tell anyone. I didn't want anyone to know. I would speak to people – other wives that I would be quite friendly with – but I would never open up to them. I would never let them know, because then I would have to say that my husband was doing something wrong. I couldn't say that. I've always had a great deal of trouble admitting to people that he's done something wrong.

It is an awful feeling, but I totally bottled it up. We just carried on. When we went to Pirbright, I had an affair with someone. I felt, 'Well, he's done it so many times, I'll put some of this hurt back on to him.' When that happened, we had just had a party to celebrate our 21st birthdays, and in hindsight we were far too young and immature to be married. We had been together since we were 16. Len had gone away on a course to Thetford and as soon as he came through the door I told him – not because I felt as if I wanted to confess all, but I wanted him to feel some of the hurt that he had put me through, and that was my way of doing it. The man wasn't anyone important to me, but I wanted to inflict a little bit of the hurt back on Len. It didn't make me feel any better afterwards. We had a dreadful time after that. I came home from work one day to find him sitting in the hallway crying his eyes out, sobbing. I felt dreadful then and I vowed that I would never hurt him like that again.

We got over it and we had Lee in February 1987. After that, Lee and the house were my main focus. My mum died and I moved to a quarter in Gillingham to be near my dad, who found it difficult to cope. I stayed there for about six months and then moved back down to Barnstaple, where Len had remained with his work. When I got back, I found out that he had been having an affair with somebody else. It was dreadful. I then had a miscarriage 14 weeks into my second pregnancy while we were at Barnstaple. I had bought maternity clothes because at three and a half months you think everything is going to be OK. It was a horrible experience and it was not nice to be in the hospital. I didn't let Len know, there was nothing he could do about it so why contact him? Someone else let him know. I thought I coped quite well with it. I thought to myself, 'Well, I've had one.'

Not long after that, we moved to Uckfield and I got pregnant with Samuel. Len went to the Falklands when Sam was born and he came back and then he went to Canada. I couldn't understand why he wanted to go away every year and not stay with the children. Now that they had got older and it was their school holiday, I didn't think it was fair that during their holiday he would spend the time in Canada. I used to think that he should be with them. Once when we lived in Aldershot and he went away, Lee was sobbing his eyes out saying, 'Please don't go.' And he just got into the taxi and went. We argued all the time. We didn't have a kind word to say to one another. Our families just thought that was us. They thought, 'Oh, that's just their way. They just bicker.' But it wasn't. There was deep-rooted hatred there because it wasn't what I wanted the marriage to be – wasn't what he wanted it to be.

He got into the PT Corps [Army Physical Training Corps] and he went from being, shall we say, 'semi-selfish' to being completely and utterly self-absorbed. It was a group who seemed to care nothing for anybody around them. I am overweight and that used to be a real bind between us. He was a real bully to try and get me to lose weight. We had awful rows. The more he told me to lose weight, the more I used to think, 'No'. It made me feel totally inferior, to the point that when we went to a Sergeants Mess summer ball, Len refused to speak to me while we were there. He refused to dance with me and didn't want anything to do with me. That must have been one of the lowest points of our marriage. I felt absolutely worthless – like a complete fool.

We went back to Crickhowell and I thought to myself, 'I'm 31 and I've got a husband who doesn't like me, doesn't love me, doesn't want to be with me. Why am I here?' We had this huge row and I asked him to leave. He left and went out to Bavaria on a hill walking and skiing course. A little while later, he phoned me up and said, 'Shall we get back together?'

I said, 'Oh, OK then. We'll give it a go.'

We were back together for a couple of months, but it was the same old thing. So again I said, 'I'd like you to leave' and he said he wanted a divorce. Soon afterwards, I met this chap who paid me attention – something I was craving for. He took me out and treated me with a degree of respect which I hadn't been used to. It didn't last very long. So I moved down to Chatham and, even though the divorce was finalised, I was still getting on great with Len's family and saw quite a bit of his mum and dad, who were very sympathetic. I found it very difficult being on my own. I felt completely alone. It got to the point where I couldn't cope any more. I wasn't working and money was very short. It was a tough time. Lee passed the 11-plus to get into grammar school and I had sleepless nights wondering how I would pay for the uniform.

Then my brother said he could give me a lift down to Wales so I could go and stay with a friend. By this time Len was out of the Army and had come back from France and was living at his mum's. I had to get away so I phoned him up and said, 'I'm going away.'

He said, 'Well, it's not very convenient.'

I thought, 'I don't care. All those times you've just upped and left me with these two children – do you think I'm going to care that it's not convenient for you?'

So I said, 'Well tough, bye.'

We got down to Wales and it transpired that my friend had been having an affair with a soldier much younger than her. For a soldier to have an affair with a married woman in the married quarters is a big 'no no'. Her husband was out in Northern Ireland with the Omagh bombing. She was hysterical because this chap was leaving and she thought she was in love with him. I talked the husband into coming home for the weekend to try and sort it out with her. So he came back for two days. Soon after his return, my friend's husband took me to the station and suddenly let rip at me, saying it was all my fault that his wife had had an affair. He was shouting at me in his car, and I was appalled that people who I thought were my friends would treat me like this. I was devastated. I was really shell-shocked coming home and I got off the train and went and picked the kids up from Len's mum and dad. Later that night he phoned me up and I burst into tears and told him what had happened. Len was just beginning to be a Christian at that time and he was very understanding. He had sort of turned his life about and become a much calmer person. And I thought, 'There must be something in this.'

We agreed to get back together and he started going to these Alpha meetings at the church. At first I thought it was just too good to be true. What they did just sounded such a load of rubbish. I didn't think it would ever last. However we decided to get married again, and we went to meet the vicar of the church where Len was doing the Alpha course. I was amazed because he was the complete opposite of what I expected a vicar to be like. His name was Glynn and he was a really nice chap. We got talking to him and he asked me if I would like to come along to the next Alpha meeting and I thought, 'I don't know about that. I don't want it rammed down my throat.' But I said, 'Hmm yes. Maybe.'

I thought about it and then, as the time approached, Len said, 'Why don't you go along? Why not go to the first one and see how you feel.' By now, Len was such a different person. Suddenly he was kind and considerate and everything he never used to be. With the plans for our re-marriage going ahead, I thought to myself, 'Am I doing the right thing?' And then I thought, 'Well, I truly believe he is a completely changed person.' Where the Alpha course was concerned I thought, 'There must be something in this, because if it could change a person like Len into what he's suddenly become, then there is something rather strong going on somewhere.' I had got a job with a firm of solicitors and I told the receptionist that I was going on this Alpha course. She was a churchgoer and bought me a little book called *Why Jesus?* I found it really interesting and thought, 'Right, I will go on that course.'

So I went along to the Alpha meeting in September 1999. It was in the vicarage and I was petrified. I thought, 'Oh no! They're going to be sitting round talking about the Bible, and I don't know anything about the Bible.' So I went along to this Alpha meeting and I was completely overawed by how friendly all the people were. I thought, 'No, people can't be this nice to you without wanting something in return.' During the talks I would sit there and find myself crying over the stories. After a few weeks of going I could really see the point and I found it quite moving.

That October my dad got taken to hospital and was very poorly. Glynn's wife, Philippa, phoned up and said, 'I hear your dad's not very well.'

I said, 'No, he's in hospital and is quite poorly.'

She said, 'Would you mind if we pray for him?'

And I said, 'Pardon?'

She said, 'Would you mind if we prayed for him?'

I was completely taken aback and said, 'That would be really kind.' I thought, 'They don't know him and they don't really know me, but they're willing to give up their time to sit and pray for this man. That's so kind.' I was only three or four weeks into the course and I was just staggered.

For the Alpha Day Away we went to somebody's beautiful house the other side of Maidstone. When we had the time of prayer, we sat there with our eyes closed and that was it. I was in floods of tears and couldn't stop. I finished the Alpha course and started going to church.

I don't go as often as I should. I don't know if I really am a Christian because I'm not as committed as Len is. He can be very outspoken, but I find it very difficult to speak openly about my faith. I believe in Jesus and the more I go to church and read the Bible, the more I find things offend me that didn't before, like when people use God's name in vain. I find that really offensive now. I like to think I am a more caring person than I used to be. I am more aware of other people's feelings. I think of Len as a true Christian because he is wholeheartedly committed, but I am on a learning curve.

At our wedding in August 2000, we had 120 people in the church. I was fine when we walked up the aisle, but when we had to say the vows, that was it. Len said his vows and his voice started to go a bit. Then, when it came to me saying mine, I was totally overwhelmed. I was sobbing so much that I couldn't speak. I felt like I wanted to lie on the floor and sob.

What difference has Jesus made in my life? Well, he has brought happiness. After being desperately, desperately unhappy at times, I am now happy and calm within. I am also, I hope, much more caring. The other day I apologised to somebody at work who I felt I had said something out of turn to. I would never have done that before. I feel I have been given another chance to be a better person.

We have got a nice relationship now – a good relationship, solid. Without God, I dread to think how awful our lives would be now – pretty grim I think. And because I know how strong Len's faith is, I don't have any worries about anything anymore. I think back to those years when he had affairs with everybody and now, hand on my heart, I can honestly say he would never do that now. He just could not live with himself if he did. God has given me back Len in the shape and form that I want him – the way he should have been when we first got married.

'I had no compassion whatsoever – neither at work nor at home. I was ruthless . . .'

Len's story

I was brought up in Chatham and have three brothers. I was a sporty type and was in all the school sports teams – football, cricket, rugby, the lot. I met Yvette, who lived nearby, when I was 16 and we started going out. In 1982, I started working in a shoe shop in Chatham as a trainee manager, when someone said to me, 'What on earth are you doing that for? Do you want to spend the rest of your life in a shoe shop? Why don't you go into the forces or something?' So at the age of 17 I joined the Grenadier Guards.

The training depot was in Pirbright, Surrey. I was in a block of about 35 guys and I was the youngest by about six or seven years. We weren't allowed out at all in the first five weeks – nor were we allowed to wear our own clothes or anything like that. It has all changed now. After my training, my first posting was to Hounslow, and in the August of the next year Yvette and I got married. We brought the wedding forward because I was posted to Northern Ireland. We were married in August 1983 and I went to Northern Ireland that October for six months.

The Household Division has got two sides to it – ceremonial duties in London (Trooping the Colour and all the rest of it) and the war role. They're very good at both. For the former, we concentrate on drill and duties outside

Buckingham Palace, Home Guard, the Tower of London, etc. For the latter, we do tactical training – weapons training and stuff like that. We moved to a married quarter in Windsor – a lovely place. Yvette was working in a bank, and for a boy of 18 I was earning good money. We had loads of money coming in and we spent it just as quickly. But my hours were horrendous. It was hard work.

From 1985-7, we were back at Pirbright, where our eldest son was born. I was a drill and weapons instructor teaching new recruits. I was power crazed. The amount of power you have over the recruits' lives is huge. My training was of the old school, where if you stepped out of line you got clobbered, not physically, but by being charged. From Pirbright we went to Fremington in North Devon, where there was an outward bound school for recruits. It was canoeing, rock climbing, caving, mountain walking – and it was a great three years. Well, it was great for me – it wasn't so great for Yvette as I was never there. It was a very tough place for these recruits to go to. We were getting them to jump off cliffs, go on runs in the sea, jump off bridges in a canoe. It was all sorts of bizarre things under the ethos of 'character development'.

I had no compassion whatsoever – neither at work nor at home. I was ruthless, with no personal fear of anything. I couldn't understand why anybody else should be scared of any of this stuff. My relationship with Yvette was terrible. We had a terrible marriage all the way through. Living in this macho tough-man environment, I went out with my mates and got drunk until the early hours of the morning. We went off with other women and Yvette just didn't fit in. I just didn't talk to her. She was the person who did the housework and washed my clothes. It was a very difficult time for Yvette.

During the next seven years, I spent three or four months each summer in the Canadian Rockies in a fantastic place called Jasper. There are fantastic white water rivers, snow and ice fields 100km away, rock climbing, rafting, mountain biking – it was my dream location. I went to Canada the first time for about four months and then I came back, and within two or three months I was sent out to the Falklands for another four and a half months. I worked in an outward bound school called Shag Cove. It was a house in the middle of nowhere on one of the less populated islands.

Men and women were flown in for their 'rest and relaxation'. They'd come over and we'd take them rock climbing and canoeing, a bit of orienteering and lots of boozing actually. There was a bar upstairs in the house.

When I returned from Canada, I decided to start training for the PT Corps. The PT Corps is physically tougher than the SAS, and includes a long line of Olympians such as Kris Akabussi. I was subsequently accepted, and after the training I was posted to Aldershot, where I became the chief instructor of the Army catering department's outdoor education wing. We would take them from Aldershot to south Wales on a Monday and stay there until Friday. So we were all away from our wives. I would only see Yvette and the kids on Saturday night and Sunday before going back again.

Eventually we moved to south Wales for two or three years. Yvette and I were going through a really rocky patch. She put up with a huge amount of rubbish from me and we separated twice. It was really horrid. Yvette stayed in the house and I went to a room in the so-called Sergeants Mess. Yvette then moved to Chatham with the children and I went to RAF Headley Court, Epsom, to train to be a sports therapist for seven or eight months. By now, we were in the process of getting a divorce. We still saw each other on the odd weekend, but the divorce came through half way through the course. I went out to the pub and celebrated with a whole group. Somebody else was getting divorced at the same time and we had a 'divorcing party'. You would sit round the table in the mess for dinner and there'd be more divorced people in there than people who were together. It was all part of the environment. Most PT Corps guys go through at least one or two wives and Yvette was just number one, so I had two or three to go yet. I scraped through the course and then I got posted to the training regiment at Winchester. It was August 1997 and I was 32.

At this stage my career was wonderful – I couldn't do anything wrong – but personally I was in pieces. I was living in the mess at that time. I was on my own. Yvette was living in Chatham, and I felt completely and utterly isolated and alone and a complete failure, even though I had all this success. It is difficult to imagine the depths of despair I was in. At night, I just got drunk all the time. I was one of these people who could go to the bar, drink six pints, get up in the morning, and then not be phased by it in the slightest because I had done it for so long.

I sometimes phoned Yvette in tears – not because I wanted to get back together, but because I didn't have anybody to speak to on a personal level. I didn't open up to my parents or my brothers. I felt I had been away for so long that I wasn't close to them. So there was Yvette – divorced, looking after two kids, with no help from me whatsoever – and I was asking her for help. I saw the kids about once a month. They seemed well-adjusted and as far as people were concerned we had a very successful divorce. We were very amicable most of the time.

Our physiotherapist at Winchester was a Christian and I used to take the mickey out of him. He was a really nice guy and I used to like being around him, but I thought he was, you know, 'touched'. I was walking out from the swimming pool one day and he was walking across with this other officer, and they said, 'Do you fancy a coffee?'

I said, 'Yeah, yeah, I think I need one.'

And we went into the rehab bit and had a coffee. They were both Christians and as we talked, they both turned to me almost at the same time and said, 'You've got a lot of problems haven't you?' I couldn't hide it. I said I had. I mentioned all the pressure that I was under at work and divorce and this, that and the other.

They said, 'We've found an answer to all of your problems and you're going to laugh if we tell you, but think about opening your heart to God.'

And I did laugh and thought, 'Here they go again!'

The next week I went skiing in Italy. I was just waiting for dinner and there was a little TV room and a library, with a line of Bibles. I thought, 'I'll read that.' I picked it up, flicked through it, stuck it in my pocket, and for the rest of that week I used to read it before I went down to dinner. And it was amazing. I read through the Beatitudes and I thought, 'This guy's got it down to a T. Everything he says is true. I'm going to try and do some of these things. I'm in a bad state and it's about time I turned my life around.' I spent Christmas that year with Yvette and the kids in Chatham. I went back to Winchester in the January and I walked into the rehab coffee room, and there were the same two guys sitting in exactly the same two chairs drinking coffee when I walked in. It seemed such an amazing coincidence. They saw my great big beaming smile and just said, 'Told you.'

Soon afterwards I left the Army. The day before I left, I was invited to work for an outdoor adventure company called Acorn Adventure, which took me to France, Spain and Italy. I read the Bible at regular intervals and would find myself in tears in my caravan thinking about things that happened before. Whenever it came to the subject of forgiveness I thought, 'I can't forgive myself, so I can't see anybody else forgiving me for what I've done.' That was a real stumbling block. I came back from Italy in September 1998 and went to live with my mum in Chatham.

Soon after moving back, I was walking up the road to see the kids when I saw this leaflet lying on the ground. It was advertising something called an Alpha course, which it explained was an opportunity to explore the meaning of life at a local church. It said, 'There is a course starting up in the local area. If you are interested just fill in the bottom of this form, send it off, and someone will get in contact with you.' It came from the church just down the road, St Philip's and St James's. At that stage I thought of myself as a Christian but I only went to church off and on. Being a bit of a 'courses person', I decided to apply for the course. Soon afterwards, I got a reply from someone called Jonathan Gardiner, who was the church's Alpha course administrator. He sent me a very nice letter saying what it was all about and when it was going to start.

At this time, I was temporarily out of work, so I went to a gym down the road and asked if they had any short-term jobs on the off chance and they said yes. The day I was due to start this new job, Yvette suddenly decided that she was going away to Wales, and she gave me the kids to look after. In the few weeks before that, she could have gone away any time and it wouldn't have bothered me. Now, suddenly, I had two kids to look after and I was running around like a lunatic. I was furious with Yvette for doing it. When she came back, I was waiting to offload all this anger that I had. But when she came back, she just burst into tears. I had all these things ready to say like, 'Don't you ever do that to me again.' But when she burst into tears I said, 'What's up?' It turned out that her trip to Wales had not been a happy time. As we sat there, I realised that all I felt was love for her. And I said, 'Shall we get back together?' It just came out.

By this time, I was going to the Alpha course every Thursday night at the local church, and I loved it. There were about 40 people there – all sitting down for dinner – and it was great. A couple called Dave and Sally were the leaders of my group and we got on really well. The talks were given by the vicar, Glynn Ackerley, and the more he spoke, the more I thought, 'Yeah, I understand that.' But my interest remained on an academic level. Then came the Alpha Day Away, which was spent in a lovely little church in Tonbridge.

After the afternoon talk, there was a time when Glynn invited the Holy Spirit to come and fill us. I saw some people fall over and I remember thinking, 'I am not going to fall over.' I had been a Guardsman so I could stand still all day without any problem. But I could understand why these people were on the floor, because the weight I had on my shoulders became so heavy that I couldn't stand up any more. It was pushing me on to my seat, so I sat down. That is when I started to cry. Glynn came over and prayed for me, and I felt completely engulfed by electricity. It was like the hugest set of pins and needles I've ever had in my life. One of my biggest problems was with forgiving myself for all the things I had done wrong. But now, all the rubbish that I'd built my life around – the drinking, the girlfriends, every-thing – was washed away and I knew I was forgiven. I felt re-born completely. It was like every bad thing I had ever done – every feeling, thought, action, deed – had gone, all gone.

It was on the Alpha Day Away when I actually became a Christian. I had changed a lot before then, but on that day my whole attitude to life changed. A few days after that, Yvette and I got engaged. We were married again in August 2000.

Jesus is now the best friend I've ever had. I can't put it into words what that means. I still have bad times, still get angry, still do things wrong – but my friend will help me out and point out when I've made a mistake, and he is always there to pick me up again afterwards. My faith has helped me with Yvette ten times over.

After a recent interview with the Army, I have just been accepted back into the PT Corps as a sports therapist. I will be going back as a completely different character. It has been a very long journey.

Len and Yvette Stanley have now moved to Winchester where Len is working at the Army Training Regiment, Winchester, where he worked before leaving the Army. They are hoping to help run an Alpha course at their local church.

5

'I took solace in the tarot cards . . .'

The story of Sam Ryan

> *Sam Ryan read tarot cards, used crystals, and attended a Spiritualist church – but she still felt that something was missing. Then one day her sister called and said, 'I've found something you must come along to . . .'*

My father turned to drink when I was very young. He was a tortured soul. I was one of five children and my mother made sure that we were clean and clothed, but there wasn't much outward display of affection, although I do know that she loved us. My mum used to take us to a big Catholic church every Sunday, but it was very much 'Be seen and definitely not heard.' My dad would go to the pub. When I was 15 I stopped going because I was going out drinking on Saturday nights. We didn't have much money.

My dad was a roofer and would have spates where he'd bring in money, but on the whole he took care of himself. This meant that my mum didn't have much money and would spend what she had on us. I loved my mum.

When I was turning 18 I met a guy called Adam on a stall in Watford market. I was on a florist stall and he was on a veg stall and love struck. It was lovely. We moved in together when I was 22 and we married four years later in 1995, the year my parents split up. Adam works in IT, which takes him away a lot, and I began looking for a new direction in my life. I was searching for something and didn't know what it was. I went along to church a few times but it felt boring. It was the same service every week. At the florist's shop where I worked I became very friendly with a customer who used to come in and talk about Spiritualism. Adam was away and I opened up to her one day and said, 'I'm a bit troubled because I'm so scared when I go to bed on my own.'

She invited me to her house, which was all dark and candlelit. Then she started doing something called 'dousing', using a crystal on the end of a chain. She explained that dousing involved using the 'auras' – all the powers from around you, like the trees and the earth – and pouring them into the crystal, allowing the crystal to answer 'yes' or 'no' to questions that you ask. The crystal would swing to the left or right for yes and no. She gave me the crystal and I tested it and it worked. I would ask silly little things like, 'Are my eyes brown?' (which they are) and it said yes. I was fascinated. The lady wasn't pushing it – it was my hand holding it. That started me thinking that there was a force out there which could be used for good. Then she said to me, 'Why don't you try a Spiritualist church?' I said I'd think about it, but I didn't go.

Instead I went back to the Catholic church – St Michaels in Watford – every now and then. I just didn't feel comfortable about the Spiritualist church. I started reading a lot of books about crystal healing and tarot cards. Then one morning I woke up and had a kind of vision. I saw a really beautiful light that was swirling and I thought, 'Oh, maybe it's time to get some tarot cards then.' So I went into this Spiritualist shop in Watford. The shop was common knowledge in the area, although I had never been in it before. Inside I found myself looking at a shelf containing cards with different pictures on them. I saw one set with a beautiful swirl and I thought, 'Oh, God is telling me to pick these cards.' So I bought them and started to use them.

At this time Adam's work really took off and he was working late and at weekends. Often I would find myself on my own and I took solace in the cards, sitting there for hours using the cards and reading books. This all took me even deeper into Spiritualism. By now I was very much immersed in this world and had a circle of friends who were all into it. Many different people heard about my interest in the cards and would say, 'Do me a reading and see what you can see.' I thought I had a special gift which could help people, so I started doing readings for people. I never charged anyone. Sometimes I would feel really quite empowered when different parts of people's lives came out. But despite that, there was always that sense of uneasiness. I can't describe it – it was really odd. My husband didn't like all the Spiritualism. I never did his cards because he wouldn't let me. While I was convinced the power came from God, he would say, 'I don't know, Sam. I'm really not happy with it. I don't like you doing it.' I used to ignore him.

In 1998, soon after the birth of our daughter Megan, I started going to the Spiritualist church. I would go to the Catholic church first, but as soon as the service finished at 11am, I would go to the Spiritualist church which was five minutes drive away. Around that time Adam and I really fell apart – not to the point where we left each other or separated, but there was a big divide. There was no communication between us. In the Spiritualist church there were about 30 to 40 people. It was very small – a hall with a little arched roof with a cross on it. When I saw the cross I thought 'Oh good, it's God.' They were very welcoming and the service began with a hymn praising God. But after that there was a lot of emphasis on getting speakers up and talking about healing and contacting people.

For example, someone would stand up and say, 'There's a woman in here who's got a friend called Katie.' And then someone would say, 'Oh, I've got a friend called Katie.' Then the first person would give a message from Katie – or perhaps Katie's brother – or perhaps someone unknown. She would say, 'I've got someone that's come forward who knows Katie and she's fine – she's happy.' I used to think, 'That's not really giving any information.' But at the same time I was intrigued that they were contacting the dead. At the time my father was very ill and I thought, 'If I haven't had a relationship with my father in this life, perhaps I can when he's dead.' I saw it as my only link to my father, and believed I had to get into training for when he died. I so wanted to give him a big hug – but he found that so difficult when he was alive. He wouldn't have a conversation with you.

For a good few months I went to Catholic mass and then to the Spiritualist church every Sunday. It was such a divide. I didn't know where I wanted to be. Then on Christmas Eve night [2000] we were sitting at my mother-in-law's enjoying a couple of drinks when there was a phone call. It was my brother calling from my mum's. He said, 'It's Dad. Come quick.' We rushed round and as we got there the ambulance-men were trying to resuscitate him. He'd had a heart attack in the kitchen. We followed the ambulance to the hospital. We could see them working on him in the ambulance, but it was no good. He died soon afterwards.

In 2001 I tried to contact him through mediumship. When you contact the dead, they're meant to be nicer. They're meant to come back as what you want – a loving father. My sister Loraine was into the same sort of thing. She happened across a friend who invited her to an Alpha course at a church in Chorleywood [Bucks]. She went to the first week and then came home and said, 'Sam, get over here next week. I've been to this church this morning and they're running an Alpha course. It's fantastic. You've got to come.' I had no idea what Alpha was. I didn't even ask her what it was, but I went the following Wednesday morn-ing – to St Andrews Church, Chorleywood. I had my daughter with me as they had a creche. There were about 25 people there of mixed ages and they were so welcoming. Their vicar gave a talk and I loved it. Then we split into our little groups.

I remember seeing this woman called Liza who was in my group. She was an older woman but she absolutely glowed and I just thought, 'I want this.' It was so lovely. So I came back the following week and I loved that too. I hadn't really thought about Jesus before – not in the way that I did through Alpha. Loraine and I went back each week and we had great debates about all sorts of things. I didn't tell Adam what I was doing. I knew he didn't like me doing the Spiritualism, so it would have been like, 'Oh dear, Sam's into something else now . . .' I didn't want him to know what I was doing, so I didn't go on the weekend. My sister went. But I continued to get so much from it – so much clarity about things. I was constantly battling with whether my Spiritualism was from God or the Devil. I told people in my group about my tarot cards, books and dousers and one woman said to me, 'Go home, get all those things and throw everything out.'

I went home, sat on my bed and looked at my dressing table. I had three candles of different sizes; I had my tarot cards in a box – wrapped in a green and white satin scarf (that was precious to me); I had my dousing things . . . I thought, 'Oh, no. What am I doing? There's nothing of God here.' I had heard that the Bible said that Spiritualism is detestable to the Lord and I thought, 'I don't want to be like that. I want to be loved by the Lord.' So I put it all into a carrier bag and threw it away with the rubbish – the whole lot, including my tarot cards. Afterwards I went downstairs and phoned Loraine and said, 'I've done it. I've got rid of them.' And she said, 'Well done!' And we chatted about Alpha.

I continued going to Alpha and as the weeks went on Jesus started to come into my life. But after the course finished I started to think, 'Have I found the right thing? What's going on?' I didn't actually buy any more cards but I started questioning what I was doing. Then I bought a Bible and I said, 'Lord, will you please tell me if you are the one to follow? With all these other religions in the world, would you please just tell me?' I opened the Bible up at random and the first thing I looked down at was, 'Do not turn to mediums or seek out spiritists, for you will be defiled by them. I am the Lord your God.' (Leviticus 19:31) I thought, 'Right, OK Lord. That's obviously you.' But I was still wavering. That's when I had a dream about getting on a train and there was darkness at one end and light at the other. I sat down and I just knew I was dead – I felt it. There were other people around me standing up. I sat facing the light because I thought, 'Great, I've been doing good things so I'll go to heaven. That's it.' But the light began disappearing and I realised I was travelling backwards towards the darkness. I was terrified and woke up screaming with the realisation that maybe I wasn't following the right thing.

After Alpha finished I went to the church at St Andrews. Adam didn't know – he went to football on Sundays. During the Alpha course my sister had given her life to Christ. She was later baptised at a Sunday service. At the service I couldn't help crying because it was so beautiful. There was just so much love in that room. People stood up and told everyone how they'd come to Christ and I thought, 'Wow, this is great!'

In the summer of 2001 I got pregnant, but after I had been carrying the baby for nearly three months I went to the hospital for a scan, and they found out it was dead. I didn't cry then but I was devastated. You're left on your own for hours waiting to see doctors and it's just horrible. Through all that I started to read my Bible more, and afterwards I started to go to St. Michaels, the Catholic church, all the time. I used to sit there and pray and pray. That was when I gave my life to God. I prayed, 'Lord, come into my life. I want you in my life. I want you here.' After that I started praying for Alpha to start in our Catholic church. I used to drop Megan at school and then I'd go and pray in church for Alpha – that it would come alive in our church. A while later I spoke to Father Chris, my Catholic priest, and he said he was planning to do it anyway! I couldn't believe it. So there was an answer to prayer.

We ran the course at St Michael's last September [2002]. We had a Holy Spirit day and it was lovely. What is happening with that parish and Alpha is fantastic. When I was planning to help on the St Michael's Alpha course I told Adam what I wanted to do, and asked him if he would look after Megan. I had prayed that he would be positive and his response was wonderful. He said, 'I've got no problems with you following your faith. You go – that's fine.'

Since becoming a Christian life has taken off for me so much. Alpha introduced me to Jesus and having Jesus in my life is such a difference. I don't think I thought of Jesus before, I just thought about God. He gives me so much love – which is what I was looking for all those years. He also gives me such a love for other people – and my relationship with Adam is so much better now, more open. I only knew the Bible as a child growing up in a Catholic family and at a Catholic school. But I didn't really understand it. Now I couldn't live without it. God definitely speaks to me through my Bible.

The difference between Spiritualism and Christianity is clear. When you take your worries to Jesus he just steps in and wipes them away. They just go and it's amazing. But with Spiritualism it's almost like you've got this horrible veil in front of you, with all your anxieties, all your hurt. It never comes clear. You try to sort it out but it never resolves itself. It goes in deeper and it makes you more worried and more anxious and it separates you from your family. When I was a Spiritualist I didn't have a relationship with anything – it was very clouded. Now I have a relationship with Jesus. I feel he's totally lifted me up in love. He comes to me as a friend when I pray about the hurt. I had so much hurt in me from the miscarriage, and my father dying, and being brought up not being able to have a relationship with him because of his violence and alcoholism.

I remember one day when all the pain of the past got on top of me. I was sitting on my bed and holding my Bible, and my husband had gone away for the weekend. I'd put Megan to bed and I just collapsed. I prayed, 'Jesus, please just come and take this pain away because I can't take any more.' After saying that I started to shake – from my toes and it went right up through my body. Then the vibration went right through to the top of my head and it lifted the pain away. And I've never been back to that state since – ever. And that is the power of Jesus in your life! He comes in and takes that pain away – fantastic. It makes me love him even more.

To anyone involved in Spiritualism I would say, 'Get out.' Go to a church where they are doing Alpha – or just go to a church and pray to Jesus and ask him to come into your life and save you. The night I gave myself to Christ I had a dream which took me back to the dream I'd had about getting on the train carriage. It was the same dream. I was led on to the train by someone and sat down in the carriage. There were people standing up and there were people sitting down, and the darkness was behind me and the light was in front of me. And I sat again on the seat looking into the light, and instead of going backwards into the darkness, the train moved forward – and I was just flooded with light.

Gram Seed

Ross Mockeridge

Christine Woodall

Claire and Peter Cooper with their children
(left to right) Grace, Samuel and Nathan

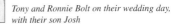

Tony and Ronnie Bolt on their wedding day,
with their son Josh

Len and Yvette Stanley with their sons
(left to right) Samuel and Lee

Ian and Nicky Morris
with their son Thomas

Sam Ryan

Steve Scott

Claude and Martin Bride with their
children *(left to right) Thibaut and Margaux*

Steven and Yolande Downes with their children (left to right) Molly, Robbie, Noah and Ezekiel

Eugene and Fran Ford with (left) Ben Price

Sarah Mansbridge

Olly Arengo-Jones

Cathy and Michael Brunton-Spall

Ben Loynes

Warren Kencroft

Deborah Field

Donna Matthews

Sam and Adam Ryan had their second child, Heather, on 9 December 2003. Sam remains a member of her local Catholic church, St Michaels, Watford. She says, 'Doing Alpha brought Adam and I so much closer.'

'I tried a wide range of spiritual paths, including astrology, Tai Chi, martial arts and a form of yoga called Kundilini.'

The story of Steve Scott

Eastender Steve Scott thought he had tried everything – astrology, Tai Chi, martial arts and a wide range of other spiritual paths. He even became interested in a type of yoga – Kundilini – which involved storing Chi energy in his navel and feet and mentally moving the energies around the body. He had relationships that didn't work out. Then a friend invited him to attend an Alpha course. This is his story:

I was born in the East End and I have lived in London all my life. I have an older brother and sister, so I am the baby of the bunch. When I was around eight or nine years old I used to go to church with relatives. Then one day we had a missionary speaking to the Sunday school and she asked what we thought she did. One of the other children said, 'Oh, you help all the little blackies.' That was the last time I went to church. I probably took it in the wrong context, but it put me off church for a long while.

When I finished college at the age of 17, I started work as a graphic artist. Most of my close friends were into music production. By the time I was 20 I was helping to run an illegal pirate radio station in the East End of London. We used to tour round doing gigs and club events – it was a 'flower-power culture' kind of thing. I realise now that there were many negative elements around me and also many bad people, but me and a handful of close friends were totally oblivious to it at the time. I didn't drink much, but I loved to dance and would be partying all night. This continued for around eight years. We were all on benefit, but would get paid cash-in-hand for DJ-ing. We used to say we were unemployable. We didn't try for jobs as we were happy doing what we were doing. We thought we were going to be really successful in the music industry, but we were just getting robbed when recording music and pressing records. We were young and naïve, and so were taken advantage of a lot of the time.

It all ended in 1995 when I turned my back on the music industry, as I slowly realised this lifestyle was not all it was cracked up to be. In 1995 I enrolled at the University of East London and did a refresher course in graphic design and a course in dressmaking, as the design field had become more computerised. I had always had a very keen interest in fashion and unique clothing, so the following year – 1996 – I embarked on a three-year course in clothing. I also got a job as a pattern cutter. I loved doing the clothing and was told I was very good at it. I did wholesale garment making, tailoring and dressmaking. In the first exam I achieved high marks which felt real good – and went on to receive another seven distinctions. I finished the course in about 1999 and then worked in the clothing industry as a pattern cutter for three years. I was working at the high end of the clothing market. I worked for the likes of Bruce Oldfield, Nicole Farhi, French Connection and others.

During these years I had girlfriends/partners – some I lived with – but I was never married. My parents didn't approve of me living with different partners, but in our era it's quite normal for people of my age to live together if they aren't married. I had long-term relationships, but after the initial 'honeymoon' period, the intensity faded out and I was never satisfied – the grass always seemed to be greener on the other side. After my last big relationship ended I did some serious soul-searching, and could see that I had always been searching for something, but I didn't know what. I was dissatisfied with my life. Then I sat down with one of my ex-girlfriends – she's like a sister to me now – and she told me her feelings/thoughts that came after the end of our relation-ship. It struck me that I'd never actually seen things from someone else's point of view before. Maybe it was just my youth and naïvity. I was always searching for the truth.

When I reached 30 years of age I told myself, 'I'm 30 – it's time to grow up. I've got to get serious with life and I'd better stop hurting people. I'd better clean up my act and sort myself out, and not be flirtatious around women.' I spent a lot of time on my own and threw myself into my work. I looked hard into everything – martial arts, astrology, many spiritual books. I also had loads of friends around me who were very spiritual people. In 1999 I walked into this funny little shop in Walthamstow. They had tarot cards and crystals in the window. The woman behind the counter said, 'What are you looking for?'

I said, 'I'm looking for clarity and love.'

She started laughing. She had a Bible on the counter and she said to me, 'What you need is in here,' pointing at the Bible.

I said, 'No, I'm not into that.' Surprisingly we spoke for about two hours.

I also investigated 'Chi energy'. They say that you can gather energy and move this energy around your body. I heard you can even have out-of-body experiences and be able to heal yourself. You can store energy in your navel and concentrate on it, and feel the energy moving around your body and things like that. I was into astrology – I read my horoscope from time to time – and Tai Chi. And I was also into a martial art – Wing Chun. There came a point in training when it becomes very spiritual and focussed.

In 2000 I started working for myself. I found the clothing industry very false in some aspects and so decided to set up on my own. I started working from the Design Centre in Walthamstow, where I met a young man, Percy Gilbert, who was another designer. He invited me to an Alpha meeting at his home. I knew it was a Christian meeting because he had put up an Alpha poster and I had read it. I invited many people from the centre but never went myself. About three weeks after Percy asked me to Alpha, I went along because I felt bad about not attending previous meetings. That was April 2001. It was a small group – about six people. Everyone was really, really nice. I was a bit sceptical at first, thinking, 'What do they want from me?' In the first part of the meeting we ate food and discussed different issues about life. We then watched the Alpha course video. It was so inspirational. I thought, 'Wow!' They gave me a lot to think about.

The strange thing was that every week issues and questions that had been going around in my head or that I'd been speaking about came up on the videos. I kept going back because I don't find that many genuine people, but I felt these people were being sincere and I had to respect that. I realised these people didn't want anything from me. I've partied with gangsters and football thugs. Not everyone will invite you into their home and be so welcoming to you when they don't know you. All this time I was having problems with my own private life. I was looking for something to help me better myself, my thoughts and my way of being.

One day I was at an Alpha meeting and I was a bit quiet. Percy asked what was wrong. I told him I was OK, but there were some problems at home. He said, 'Would you like me to pray for you?'

So I said, 'All right.'

They said some prayers and told me how I could pray to Jesus and ask for forgiveness, and ask him to come into my life. I thought, 'That's not hard. I can do that.' I did pray for forgiveness and I invited Jesus into my life and I meant it. I had tried to love as much as I could love, and to be as forgiving as I could possibly be in life, but it still wasn't enough to overcome what I was up against. So if help came in the shape of Jesus I was prepared to say, 'Yeah, OK.' I think it was a couple of days later someone said to me, 'I've heard you've become a Christian.'

I said, 'Have I?' It took a few days to sink in because my impression of a Christian was someone in a grey robe with a wooden cross around their neck, walking the street looking really humble and dismal.

The day before the Alpha Day Away I was at my flat. I got down on my knees and said a prayer again and asked

God for more forgiveness. Then I started thinking about the people I knew in all the clubs and parties. I said to God, 'Well, you've saved me, but what about all the people still out there in the clubs? I don't want to be saved if my friends can't be saved.' I got very emotional. So that night something hit me and I was forgiving everyone, and was trying to pray for everyone that I could possibly think of. I was crying and I hadn't cried for years – not since I was in my mid-teens when I had witnessed a friend of mine getting killed. That night I couldn't go to sleep. The Alpha Day Away was on my mind. It seemed as though I pressed my shirt four times, ironed my trousers twice, polished my shoes, then polished them some more . . . It was like I had a big interview or meeting. I needed to sleep, but I couldn't get to sleep.

The next day I got to Percy's early. I said to him, 'I bet you thought I wasn't going to come.'

And he said, 'No, I knew you'd come.'

At that stage I was the only new person left on the Alpha course. There was just me, Percy and his helper, Yenni. There were about three other churches at the Alpha Day Away. I really liked the guy giving the talks and at one stage he came and prayed over me. The Holy Spirit came into me, and it was almost as if whatever was inside me was being taken out and I was being cleansed. My chest was up in the air – like I was being pulled up. It was very powerful. I was panting and couldn't breathe properly. I was coughing but I wasn't feeling ill. It was like there was something inside me that needed to come out. I think I was there 45 minutes later, still coughing and panting. I don't know how long it was. It came to a point where I started saying to myself, 'Enough now.' It was like the power was so intense that I couldn't take any more. It was an unbelievable experience.

After that I started going to church regularly. I attended the River of Life ministry in Bethnal Green. Jesus has made a difference because I have an assurance that everything is and will be all right. I pray every day. I find myself in prayer so much of the time. I wouldn't have done that before. I wouldn't have known what to pray about. Now I know that there's a promise there and God doesn't lie. There are so many people who would love to be in the position I'm in, if they had the knowledge of how to get there. So what Alpha's doing is great. It needs to be done more. So many people want to be at peace with themselves and God. Before I only knew half the story. I used to think that if you wanted to get close to God, you had to go to church and do whatever the vicar said. It's only when I found out that I could have a relationship with Jesus that it brought me along.

I read the Bible now. I didn't do that before. I used to try – maybe pick it up once every three years – but I'd just end up getting more confused. Now I'm inspired by it, because I can relate the Bible to today and the situations around me. I'm going to church every week. Now I'm just trying to get my friends and family into it.

Steve Scott is now a member of 'The River of Life Ministry' in Bethnal Green. He started a Christian Youth group in September 2002 (along with Percy Gilbert and another friend), attended on average by 30 young people from the area. Steve also runs a small Alpha course within Tower Hamlets.

6

'I said, "God, I'm so desperate . . ." '

The story of Claude & Margaux Bride

> *The story of little Margaux Bride hit the headlines all
> over the country in spring 2001, when her need for a
> heart transplant was complicated by the lack of
> donated organs as a result of the Alder Hey scandal.
> Amid all the trauma, baby Margaux's mother, Claude,
> was invited on an Alpha course at Holy Trinity
> Brompton by her next door neighbour. Here Claude
> tells the extraordinary story – both of Margaux and
> her new relationship with God:*

I was brought up in France in the Catholic faith, but after
leaving home at 18, I stopped attending church services
regularly. I used to go, like many people, at Christmas and
special celebrations: christenings, communion, confirmation
and weddings. I met my husband Martin at a party in Paris

after my best friend said to me, 'Oh, I've met this very nice Englishman, whom you have to come and meet. I have a feeling you might like him.' And I did. We married in 1996 and two years later – in June 1998 – our son, Thibaut, was born. By then we were living in London, where Martin had been posted.

I became pregnant with Margaux in 1999 and all the worry started at my 20-week scan. I arrived confidently at Chelsea & Westminster Hospital. There was no serious medical history in our family and we had a healthy toddler, so there was nothing to prepare me for what happened next. The radiographer looked at the screen and then said she wanted to discuss something with her colleagues. Then two radiographers joined her and all of them looked at the screen with puzzled expressions. Finally they said that my baby had very serious heart problems. I left there in tears feeling lost and helpless.

A week later I saw a consultant. He told me there was some chance that the defects could be repaired through open heart surgery, but even then there would be a lot of risk involved and the baby may not survive. I was given the choice of having a termination, but I could feel this baby kicking inside me, and I said, 'No way. I want to give the baby a chance.' I was convinced that I would have had the feeling I had killed my baby and would have felt remorse all my life.

On 31 January 2000 Margaux was born. She looked so lovely, normal – we couldn't believe there was anything wrong with this lovely little girl. She was just perfect. But just as they had predicted, she was very unwell. She was transferred immediately to the specialised unit of the Brompton Hospital. The very next day she went through major open-heart surgery with a 50 per cent chance of survival. The surgery went on for six hours and it was a very long time to wait. She survived the surgery – but she didn't recover too well and that operation only gained them some time. She stayed in hospital for the whole of February and at the beginning of March she had more open-heart surgery. After that we took her home, but three months later it all flared up again and she was admitted again.

By then she was on the verge of death and I was desperate. I had planned to have her christened by my cousin, who is a Catholic priest in the south of France. But Margaux didn't leave us time. The surgeon said, 'We're going to operate tomorrow and there is only a one-third chance that she may survive.' It was awful. So we had her christened at once without any preparation by a Catholic priest – organised by the hospital. But as the priest had to leave quickly after the christening, I was left frustrated with all my desires for prayer . . . I was in tears when he left. So I called my very nice neighbours in Tooting – Michael and Ursula Wright – who I knew were regular churchgoers and said, 'Could you help me to pray for her?'

They said, 'Of course!'

They also mentioned that the chaplain at the Royal Brompton Hospital came from their church, Holy Trinity Brompton, and asked if they could organise for him to meet me. I said 'Yes,' gratefully.

The next morning at 8am, just before the surgery, the chaplain, Jez Barnes, arrived to meet me. He came up with a nice smile and immediately when I saw him I thought, 'Ohhh – he seems nice and friendly.' He started to chat to me like a normal person – he didn't start talking to me about God straightaway, but asked questions about Margaux and our family. After a while he said, 'Would you mind if I read a passage from the Bible?'

That was amazing because that's exactly what I wanted and I said, 'Oh no, no, please do.' And he read the passage about how Jesus raised Jairus' daughter.

Then he said a very simple prayer – and I repeated it afterwards – something like, 'Jesus, we are gathered today with Claude, the mother of Margaux, who is going to undergo major surgery in a few hours. We do ask you to protect her, to look after her, to watch over and to guide the doctors, nurses and surgeons who are going to perform the surgery. We also ask you to give strength to her and Claude and Martin who are desperate, and to strengthen them in their sorrow and give them hope. Please God, hear our prayer and keep Margaux in your hands . . . We ask you this in the name of Jesus.' And that was it.

The operation was on July 5 and Margaux was so unstable during the surgery that the surgeon didn't even manage to finish everything. She was really critical that week and was kept on a life support machine, not only heavily sedated but also paralysed and cooled down, like in an artificial coma. Jez came every day to pray with me and that was a wonderful comfort. She became so unstable that we thought she was going to die. The doctors said, 'There's nothing else we can do,' and they suggested that we say goodbye to her. But we kept praying and she stabilised a bit – and became well enough to support further surgery on July 11. Her recovery did not last long however.

In November she needed more open-heart surgery, and although she survived that surgery one more time, it didn't solve her problem in the long-term. That was when the doctors said, 'We've done absolutely everything. Her only

chance of survival now is a heart transplant.' Soon after that
Michael and Ursula invited me to supper at their house, and
they showed the video of Nicky Gumbel's talk, 'Christianity: Boring, Untrue and Irrelevant?' I was extremely
impressed, but felt that with a very sick baby I did not have
any time to do an Alpha course. Then at the beginning of
January, Margaux was again critically ill and was again
admitted into Intensive Care. That is when we decided to go
for a heart transplant. It was Margaux's only chance.

We had a nanny for Thibaut and Margaux, Jo Greenway,
and as it happened, she had been on an Alpha course a few
years before and was a Christian. At this time – January
2001 – she saw I was really stretched. Martin was away in
Philadelphia, USA, where he was doing a training course for
six weeks, and my father was dying from cancer in a hospital bed in France. I was so tired and irritable – I was just desperate. So without saying a word, Jo just left an Alpha leaflet
on the corner of the table in the kitchen. I read it and
thought, 'Oh! The Alpha course is on Wednesday mornings
– and that's my only day off!' Since September I had been
back at work (for Standard & Poor's – an American financial company in London) and was working four days a week
– every week day except Wednesdays. Holy Trinity Brompton – which was where the Alpha course was held – is next
door to Margaux's hospital. I thought, 'If I go to this Alpha
course for two hours Margaux will hardly notice my absence
from hospital . . .' (she was heavily sedated and ventilated)
'. . . and I'm desperate. I need to find meaning in my life, to
have a direction.'

So I went to the Alpha course in January 2001. As soon
as I arrived I felt uplifted. Everything seemed to make sense
to me. I started to read *Questions of Life* and even began

going to the church on Sundays with Thibaut, as Margaux was still in hospital. Thibaut, who was three years old, enjoyed the morning family service tremendously. I think I only survived that period because of the Wednesday morning at Alpha and Sunday in church. I looked forward to it every week and it kept me alive during this time.

Meanwhile Margaux was very, very critical and there were no organs being donated to enable transplants to take place. There had just been an awful scandal in Liverpool called the 'Alder Hey', where doctors were charged with holding on to organs without the agreement of parents – it was awful. And then people started to get confused between organs for research – which is one thing, and organs which are still living and used to save lives through transplantation – something very different.

While we were waiting, two babies on the waiting list died in front of our eyes, and the big likelihood was that Margaux would die as well. The Wednesday of that week I went along to Alpha and we were asked if we were prepared to give our life to Jesus. Although I prayed sincerely, I did not give my life to Jesus during the Alpha session. But as I was leaving HTB walking back to hospital, I had a compelling thought. And I said to God, 'I know I ought to be prepared to give you my entire life without asking for anything, but this is beyond my strength. I feel like Thomas, the apostle, who needed to see in order to believe. I give you my life Jesus – but please save Margaux.'

When I arrived at the hospital that day, Sir Magdi Yacoub, Margaux's surgeon, came to visit her. He said she did not have much time to wait and that's when we talked about an appeal to the press to draw the attention of people to organ donation. I followed his advice and *The Times* printed an article I wrote about Margaux. I was then approached by other media. After that I began to receive letters and messages from hundreds of people all over the world. I received one message from an Alpha group in South Africa who said they were praying for Margaux. Another from Australia and France. It was amazing. Most of the messages came from the UK of course, but everyone in their letters said they were praying for Margaux. This affected me even more than anything else. I had never doubted that there was a God, but now I started really to feel him all around us. I had a feeling that God was carrying Margaux – and carrying me – through this.

The Alpha Weekend was on March 9 and I had paid and planned to go. Although Margaux was in Intensive Care, and I was spending most of my time at her side, I felt I needed the lifeline. But on March 7 and 8, Margaux had two consecutive cardiac arrests where her heart stopped. I was holding her hand and I saw the whole thing. The doctors were really good, but they had to shock her heart with an electric device three times before it started again. I asked a nurse to call my friend, Theresa Morrish, another mother of a long-term patient, Gabriel. She arrived, took my hands and said, 'Shall we pray?'

I said, 'Yes' in tears, and I prayed and said, 'Please God, I'm going to ask you one more time, could you please save Margaux . . .'

And her heart started again after the third time. The following day around the same time her heart stopped again. By now I didn't know what to pray any more. The doctors resuscitated her again but said things were so desperate that she could die at any moment. I just said, 'God, I'm so desperate, desperate, desperate. Shall I pray for her to be released from her suffering quickly and to go to heaven, or shall I pray for a miracle to happen? Maybe I shouldn't hold on any more?' I had stopped hoping that Margaux could be saved in the long-term. Since there had not been a single suitable organ for that age group in the last three months in the whole of the UK, what were the chances that one would turn up now for Margaux at the eleventh hour? I called my Alpha group leader and was crying on the phone to her. I said, 'I'm not coming to the Alpha Weekend tomorrow because Margaux has had a second cardiac arrest. It's terminal – I have to stay at her bedside.'

And she said, 'Of course, I understand. We'll pray for you.'

And then I said, 'You know Shirley, I'm so desperate I don't even know what to pray for any more.'

And she said, 'You have to pray to be guided by God. Just say to God that you're also desperate, and you don't know what to pray for and you need him to guide you.'

And that's what I did. I fell asleep praying to be guided and to receive a sign from God to show me the way. The following morning when I woke up, I felt really calm for the first time in many months. I went to hospital and even bought a toothbrush on my way in, just in case I would have to spend the night there. I had never been so relaxed before. Then when I arrived at the hospital, Margaux's doctor, Joan Larovere, came to meet me at the door of the Intensive Care Unit and said, 'Claude, please come into my office – we think we've got a suitable donor for Margaux!'

I thought, 'This cannot be coincidence. It has to be divine intervention, because last night I prayed for a sign, and this is the best sign I could ever hope for!'

The donor was a little 15-month-old Norwegian girl

called Hilda Marie, who was born with hydrocephalus. She died, tragically, while in hospital on a ventilator, which meant that it was possible for her organs to be donated. The parents had never read *The Times* and were not influenced by our story. They said she was a very lively, beautiful baby, and they wanted their tragedy to be useful for someone. The Royal Brompton Hospital flew a helicopter to Norway with a surgeon team and the operation happened that Friday night. It was wonderful to know that everyone was praying on the Alpha Weekend, which had just started. Also, just before the operation, Jez Barnes and Nicky Lee from Holy Trinity came and prayed with me for Margaux. They prayed for God to protect Margaux during the surgery, and said other prayers too, for the family of the donor, who had tragically lost their little baby.

Immediately after the transplant was over, Professor Yacoub said they were satisfied. More time passed and she started putting weight on and breathing on her own. She even began to be fed orally. She became alert and a very happy baby. Through this time I continued going to Alpha and even started helping on the next Alpha course. I went on the Alpha Weekend in May as a helper, which was wonderful, and found I loved praying for other people. Doing Alpha made Jesus more like a human person to me and a friend. In the past I used to pray, 'Our Father who is in heaven,' but it was almost like an automatic move. Now I pray with my own words. It has made such a difference in the way I pray and relate to Jesus. I didn't even know I could speak to him like that, so it has completely changed my understanding.

On May 15, 2001, Margaux left the Royal Brompton Hospital to go home. She was 15 months old and had spent a year in hospital. A few months later we all moved to Paris, where Martin had a new job. Now Margaux is much, much better. She has started to walk and to behave like any other little child. If you saw her, you could never imagine what she's gone through. She is so full of life – even cheeky. She loves to do jokes. She likes to make bubbles in her bath. She needs to take drugs at regular hours every day all her life – it's difficult, it's an inconvenience. But she is lovely, she is lovely. I always thank God for his miracle ... and I even thank God for giving me that child and not another child, because I think she is wonderful and changed my life. I wouldn't have swapped our Margaux with a healthy Margaux. It's the Margaux we have and we love her ... She continues to have occasional operations and the doctors are watching her carefully.

The fact that the transplant occurred the precise night the Alpha Weekend was starting, was another sign for me. I couldn't help thinking that all our prayers must have helped. If I had any doubt before that God existed – and any doubt about the power of prayers – those doubts were certainly dispelled. It is an amazing triple coincidence that a potential donor came forward, not only at the very last minute after Margaux's consecutive cardiac arrests, but also the night my Alpha Weekend was starting and the week Martin had just returned from the States. So he was at our side again when the transplant occurred after six weeks of absence. Plus I remembered my promise to God. I had given him my life but asked him to save Margaux. And he did! In any case even if I will never be able to prove that prayers helped Margaux, one thing is certain: they certainly helped me, her mother, to cope and feel uplifted throughout the most difficult time of my life.

I want to put God first in my life, but I feel I haven't done it quite yet. It's something I am praying for and hoping for. The one thing I would love to do is to attend a local mid-week prayer group here in Paris, where we now live – so I am looking for that.

Margaux's health continues to improve and she started school in September 2003. Claude says, 'I pray to God every single day to thank him for saving Margaux and for being so present in our lives now. I really feel that I have a real relationship with God now. I speak to him, ask him for advice, pray, and he is a real companion.'

'I only went on the Alpha course to be disruptive.'

The story of Steven Downes

Steven Downes of Cromer, Norfolk, went on an Alpha course to stop his wife, Yolande, being 'brainwashed'. During the course they were told by doctors that their unborn child had Cystic Fibrosis. Their Alpha group offered to pray...

I was born in Norwich and moved to Cromer, Norfolk, when I was four years old and I've been living in Cromer ever since. My parents were teachers and I've got lots of good memories from my childhood. There was plenty of love in our house. We weren't Christians. I think we used to go to church for weddings, funerals and Christmas day, but that was it. My father was very anti-church, and both my brother and I picked that up and formed an opinion that there wasn't a God, and that Christians were really making a big mistake. The only positive aspect of Christianity in my life was my best friend, Alistair, who became a Christian on a beach mission in Cromer when he was about nine years old. I used to take the mickey out of him relentlessly, and in fact I was a bit unpleasant about it really.

Throughout school and college I played a lot of sport and never really thought about God at all – only in a negative way. When I was in my second year at college I applied for a training post at the Eastern Daily Press in Norwich. I kept getting asked back as the selection got smaller and finally they offered me one of the training posts.

When I finished the training in January 1993, I was posted to the office at Lowestoft as a junior reporter. I did a year there and then led a fairly nomadic lifestyle going around the county to different offices, until I returned to Cromer when I was 22. I really liked Cromer because I knew the people and it was easy for me to find stories. I worked hard when I was at work, but the rest of the time my thoughts were on two things: football and drinking.

I had a very busy social life and I didn't have much moral control over my life – I basically lived for myself and I didn't think too much about other people's feelings. That went on for about 18 months, until I met Yolande. She was part of the darts team at the pub, and as I was normally propping up the bar we got to be quite good friends. Yoly was married, but sometime later she and her husband broke up. After that, she called me and asked if I'd like to go round for a meal. We got on really well and we decided to start seeing each other more regularly, and it just snowballed from there. Yolande already had two children, Molly and Robbie. We decided very quickly that we wanted to live together, and within six weeks I proposed to her.

I decided I wanted to get married in a church. As Yoly had been married before we couldn't get married in the Anglican church, so we went to the Methodist church in Cromer where my grandparents had worshipped. I couldn't explain why, but I felt it was right to get married in a church. I didn't want a registry office. We had to have a talk with the minister of the church, which was a bit of an ordeal. We both had things from our past that we didn't necessarily want to confront. The minister was aware that we didn't have any faith, but he was still happy to marry us, which was good. Yoly said we couldn't get married in a church and not attend it. She felt it was hypocritical. So we started to go to church together before the wedding. In the end, I didn't go that often as I had Sunday league football. Yoly would take Molly and Robbie to church while I went off to football. I wasn't bothered by her going to church because I didn't think she was in any danger of being converted. I just thought, 'She'll stop going once we're married.' The times I did go to the church I can't say I listened to a word of it, but I remember thinking, 'It's nice the people are so friendly.' And we got on really well with the minister.

We got married in May 1998. It was a wonderful day and the service was nice – although I didn't take a lot of notice of that part of it. We went away on our honeymoon, and quite soon afterwards we got an invitation through the post from Keith, the minister, to a course called Alpha. Yoly looked at it and said, 'I think I'm going to go on this.'

I was absolutely horrified. I thought we had got away from the church. I had no intention of being converted and I had no intention of my wife being converted. At this point my real feelings about Christianity came to the surface. I thought it was just a crutch for people to lean on. There was no truth in it, there was no God, and Jesus was just a nice man who lived and died. Yoly decided to go along with a friend of hers called Sara, and I suddenly got worried that she might get converted and so I thought, 'Right, I'll go along with her.' My sole purpose of going was to be a disruptive influence, to ask lots of awkward questions and to make sure that they didn't brainwash my wife. It was a joint Alpha course held between the local Anglican and Methodist church.

We went to an Alpha supper party first and watched the introductory video called, 'Christianity: Boring, Untrue and Irrelevant?' That first evening I remember feeling welcome and interested. There were about seven of us in the group and we would meet up in someone's home, have coffee, watch the video, have another coffee and then a chat. I watched the video and thought, 'Yeah, it's quite interesting.' As the weeks progressed we found ourselves getting really into it and talking about real issues. It was very relaxed and you felt you could ask anything you wanted. Tim was the Anglican curate running our group and I really related to him.

By this time Yoly was pregnant, and we went for the routine 20-week scan at the Norfolk and Norwich Hospital. We were so excited and couldn't wait to see our baby. But when we got there and looked at the screen, we received a real bombshell. They told us that the baby had Cystic Fibrosis. They said it had an ecogenic bowel, which meant that the bowel was clogged up with mucus – a sure sign of Cystic Fibrosis. That knocked us sideways as you can imagine and we just cried. We went home and then came back three days later for another scan, which revealed the same. We then asked for the sex of the baby because we thought, 'We can't keep calling it "It".' It was a boy.

The consultant then told us about all the implications of having a baby with Cystic Fibrosis and so, after a lot of soul searching and a lot of tears, we decided that we were going to have a termination. We didn't want to knowingly cause a child of ours to suffer. It was turmoil for us. We had bonded with the baby by then, and at night I would be lying in bed with Yoly and you could feel him kicking. It wasn't an 'It'. It was a baby and it was our baby.

At the next hospital appointment Yoly took her overnight bag, because we thought she was going to stay and have the termination. We sat in a room with a consultant and he left us to make the final decision. We looked at each other and suddenly decided that we would have the baby after all. We thought, 'We've got good in-laws, we've got good friends. If anyone can cope then we can.' The relief was enormous. It was such a weight off our shoulders. We knew then we had made the right decision. We thought, 'We've got to give this child a chance.' In the meantime we had had a week off the Alpha course because of all the trauma. We were also worried about telling them about the termination, because we thought they would be so against it. We then heard that people in the church were praying for us, which I thought was very kind. I guess in my heart I thought it was futile, but at least they were trying to do something, trying to give us some support, even if it was via an entity that I didn't believe existed. Then one night I had a dream. I dreamt that

I was having an argument with Yoly about the name of our child. She wanted to call him Malcolm but I wanted to call him Ezekiel. I woke up in the morning and told Yoly about the dream and she said, 'What's Ezekiel?'

I said, 'I don't know, I've never heard of it.'

At the next Alpha night we asked Tim about it and he said, 'Oh, it's a biblical name. Ezekiel was an Old Testament prophet.'

He said the name meant 'strength of God' and we thought, 'Well, that's nice, because if there is a God we need his strength at the moment.'

Then another strange thing happened. Yoly and I went looking around Christian bookshops for Bibles, and every Bible we opened we kept opening it out at the book of Ezekiel. It's not the most well-thumbed book of the Bible, so it was quite surprising.

We then started to think, 'Perhaps this is God. Perhaps God gave us the dream and is causing us to open the Bible at Ezekiel. Perhaps we're being told to give the name Ezekiel to our son.' Tim then told me that he had prayed for me saying, 'Lord, please speak to Steve in a dream, do something he can't deny.' We worked out that he had prayed that the day before my dream, which seemed quite a coincidence. While we thought Ezekiel was an unusual name we started to grow to like it, and decided that that is what we would call our baby. We were then about three-quarters of the way through the Alpha course and we were loving it. We would come home from the course and sit up in bed for an hour with a Bible looking at various things.

One of the last nights of Alpha was held at our home because we couldn't get babysitters. It was wonderful to have everyone round because by then we were all very close. It was the talk on healing and at the end Tim said, 'Would you mind if I pray for you and your unborn baby?' We all stood up in a circle and Yoly stood in the middle and Tim prayed for her. He prayed that God would protect her and the baby and our family. At the end she said that she had felt an unnatural heat going through her body. I was really moved, although I was a little bit worried that the neighbours might see and think we were part of some kind of cult. I felt a little bit strange praying like that, though. I didn't know you could have a one-to-one relationship with God.

We then had another appointment at the hospital for yet another scan. The lady put the ultrasound on and we looked at the screen. She was clearly looking for something. Then after a while she said, 'Well, the mucus has probably spread out a little bit, as it's not so clogged up.' We then had scans every few weeks and each time they would say, 'Well, it looks like a normal scan.' We then started getting very excited and thought, 'Maybe he hasn't got Cystic Fibrosis very badly. Perhaps he's just got asthma.'

The Alpha course then came to an end and we felt empty. We had loved the course so much and we thought, 'Oh no, what do we do now?' Yoly and I then sat down together one evening and had a chat, and decided that we did believe in God. We said, 'Let's do it. Let's become Christians.' It was quite a moving night. It was lovely. The next day we phoned Tim up and said, 'We want to make a commitment to follow Jesus. Can we come around to see you?' We went to Tim's house and after lunch we went into his office. He then said, 'Try to think of things that you want to ask forgiveness for. You can either say them out loud today, or go home and think about it and ask God in your own time.' We then said a prayer of commitment, asking God for forgiveness, declaring our belief in Jesus and giving our lives to him. There were no thunderbolts or lightning – just a real sense of peace.

Before that, we had been very embarrassed about telling people we were doing the Alpha course, but afterwards we got very excited telling people about Christianity. We got this passion to read Christian books, to learn more about God and just to open the Bible and to learn, learn, learn. Tim had said to us, 'The way to develop a relationship with God is to pray and to speak to him.' So we started praying together. It was so nerve-wracking sitting in bed together the first time, saying, 'Who's going to go first?' We did feel a bit silly at first, but it was good and we knew it was right. In our early prayer life we prayed a lot about the baby. We would just pray, 'Oh please God, don't let him suffer too much.'

If someone had said to me when I got married, 'In a year's time you're going to be sitting in bed with your wife reading the Bible and praying,' I would have probably sworn at them. That's another thing – when I became a Christian, I stopped swearing. It wasn't a conscious decision – it just happened. I also gave up Sunday football because I wanted to go to church and be with my family. We decided to find a different church because the Methodist church wasn't really set up for a family with young children.

We spoke to Keith and he recommended the Anglican church around the corner from us, called St Martin's. We went there on Christmas day and the people made us feel so welcome. It's a really lovely little church – very intimate, very friendly. Yoly then went into labour and we went to the hospital. We were still expecting that Ezekiel would have some form of Cystic Fibrosis, but we weren't sure to what degree. At the birth there were two midwives and two consultants there ready to take him to the special unit and get him on a ventilator. But when he was born he cried, which was a good sign. They took some blood straight from the umbilical cord. We then had to wait for him to empty his bowel, because normally it takes a long time for babies with Cystic Fibrosis to go to the toilet, because their bowel is so congested. But he went pretty quickly. They then took some blood out of his heels which had to be sent away for tests.

The consultants and the paediatrician were looking at him and saying, 'Well, there's not much wrong with you, is there?' One of the midwives asked us what we were going to call him and we said Ezekiel. She asked what it meant and we said, 'strength of God'. When Yoly went out to have a bath, I held Ezekiel and prayed for him and dedicated him to God. We then went home and had to wait a couple of weeks for the final test results to come through. We then got a letter from the hospital saying, 'We are pleased to let you know that your baby doesn't have Cystic Fibrosis.' At that point all the tension came out and we just cried. The relief of opening that letter and getting it in black and white was a very emotional time for us.

Since then we have changed so much and God has done so much for us. We feel really blessed. We have such a love for people. We find we don't get miserable with life and we cope with things a lot better. We started going every week to St Martin's. I got involved with a Bible study group and started to look into the Bible in much greater depth – I got such great excitement from that. Now God is using us to meet with people who aren't Christians, that are a similar age to us with children. We encourage them to go on an Alpha course, and get them along to the church toddler group and to church. For a while we were the only young family at St Martin's, but now there are five young families that regularly come. There are now about 60 women and children at the Thursday toddler group. It all seems to have grown out of what God has done in our life.

Yoly has a ladies group that she goes to on a Friday night, which has grown and taken off. There have been healings there and all sorts of things.

We started to pray with the children at night and they liked that. We also pray at meal times – it's become a part of their lives now. We're trying to make God a living God in their lives. I don't want it to be something that will put them off. They are excited about it and their prayers are much lovelier than ours.

We couldn't go back to how it was, no way. I would feel completely empty without Jesus in my life. Although obviously we have our ups and downs and we don't pray as often as we should, we know that he's there.

Steven and Yolande Downes now attend Sheringham Baptist Church. Steven helps with the Cromer Beach Mission each summer and they are both involved with youth work.

7

'Jesus has turned our family round.'

The story of Eugene & Fran Ford

Eugene Ford married twice and had eight children before suddenly leaving home to start a new life with the wife of his best friend. Some years later, his 16-year-old stepson, Ben, went on an Alpha course and Eugene was invited along. It was the beginning of an extraordinary change in his life:

Eugene's story

I left school when I was about 14 without any qualifications and got a job in a factory. I got married to my first wife when I was 18. We had several homes before settling in Chemsley Wood, just outside Birmingham. We had four children: Mark, Eugene, Karen and Tracey. We were married for 18 years until one day in 1976 I just left. I told her that I didn't love her and I couldn't lie to her any more. The truth was that I had been having an affair with a girl at work, called Alison. About a year afterwards, Alison and I got married. We married in a registry office in Lichfield and went on to have another four kids: John, Brendan, Richard and Ryan. We were married for 12 years. I was a very bombastic person. It was like, 'I'm the man, I'm the gaffer, I wear the trousers.' I was quite a strict dad. My children knew where they stood, and if they did anything wrong, they could expect a bit of a clip round the ear. The children from my first family were all pretty grown up by this stage.

In 1982, I got made redundant after 18 years, and I started to get pretty dissatisfied with everything. I kept saying to myself, 'Is this it?' I started to feel like a loner whenever I went anywhere with Alison. This sort of dissatisfaction and loneliness creeps up on you. You sort of feel that you're not part of everything, there's something missing. My relationships with my children were fine, and also with the children from my first marriage. They were the joy of my life, but I still felt this detachment from everything and a growing dissatisfaction. I then had an affair with my neighbour, Fran.

She and her husband Karl had moved into our road in about 1986 with their three children. They lived opposite us. We all became good friends and I was sort of Karl's best friend. Fran and I started looking at each other and thinking about each other in about 1991. I remember one day she came across from their home, and came up to me and said something like, 'I know exactly what I want, but it's up to you what you want to do.' We then started seeing each other. After about six or seven months I got tired of telling lies to my wife and Fran's husband, and I decided to do something about it. One day I had been drinking at home and was a bit

drunk. Fran had arranged to pick Alison up that night from
the chip shop where she worked, and I decided to go along
for the ride. On the way there I said to Fran, 'I'm not going
back.'

She said, 'What do you mean?'

I said, 'I'm not going back home. That's it.'

She said, 'Oh, don't be silly.'

When we got there we found Alison, and I sort of started
an argument with her all at once. I said I didn't love her any
more. I'd been trying to get it out for ages.

She said, 'Oh, you're drunk. Come on, Fran, let's go.
Let's leave him here.'

They went and left me there at the back of the chip shop.
I was just in my flip-flops and shorts. It was about 12 midnight. It didn't matter though because I was drunk. I sat down
and propped myself against the wall. I hoped Fran would
come back and she did. She said, 'What's the matter?'

I said, 'I don't want to go back home. We're going. Are
you coming?'

She went, 'What about the kids?'

I said, 'We can sort that out after.'

So we went. We only had a fiver between us and we
decided to head to Wales and stay there until everything
calmed down, and we could get things sorted. Unfortunately
we only got as far as Shrewsbury – 50 miles away – when
the car broke down and we had to spend the rest of the night
in the car. Half way through the night the police pulled up –
Karl and Alison had called them and asked if we were all
right. When they left it suddenly dawned on us what we
were doing, and we then sat up talking for a few hours,
trying to sort everything out together and work out what we
were going to do.

The following morning we walked to Shrewsbury, which was about seven miles away. We got to the town centre and Fran sold her wedding ring to get some money. She only got £35. As I was still only wearing shorts and flip-flops, we went into a charity shop and I got a pair of trousers, shoes and socks. We then decided to go back to Tamworth – near our homes – to see if we could go to some local loan agencies to get some money. To get there, we hitched a ride with a lovely lady. We told her what had happened and she was actually very sympathetic. As it turned out, she had done a similar thing about five or six years before, and was now living in Llangwynadl in Wales. She'd remarried since then. She said she knew how it felt, and said, 'If you want any help, here's my address. If you do decide to come to Wales, look me up.'

When we got back to Tamworth we tried to get some more money. Fran went to Providence (a loan agency) and managed to borrow £60. We then went to Birmingham – New Street Station – and got the train to Wales and went to stay with this woman in Llangwynadl. We stayed with her for about four or five nights, and then moved into a caravan she had on her farm. We lived there for about a month and then she found us a static caravan down the lane, where we lived for another four or five months. During that time, I was trying to sort out somewhere for us to live through Tamworth Council back in Birmingham. Eventually we were given a one-bed place in Tamworth. We lived there for about a year, and then we were given a bigger place the following year.

In 1993, Fran and I got married and we moved into a bigger house – the house we live in now. Fran's three boys then came to live with us, because Karl didn't have a big enough place for them to live in. By this time we were both actually feeling pretty low and things were quite hard. Although it was obviously our choice to get together, we'd both lost our homes and all our possessions, and so we had to pick ourselves up from nothing, and try and get started in our new life together. It was also hard to cope with all the devastation we had caused. We had caused a lot of hurt to both our immediate family and lots of other people: our parents, brothers, sisters, children. Fran's dad didn't speak to her for five years. I walked up to the local church a couple of times, but the doors were locked and I sort of took that as a bit of a sign.

In 1995 I had a heart attack and I was diagnosed with diabetes and asthma, which meant I couldn't really do much work and Fran was looking after the kids, so we were quite poor. One day Fran and I noticed an advertisement in the paper for a stall in a local indoor market. It proved to be a nice corner stall and we thought we could open a hair salon there, because Fran is actually a qualified hairdresser. We decorated it and put sinks in and created a lovely salon. We then had a lovely life. We did just three days and we were doing £300-£400 a week – absolutely glorious. It was a lot of money for us and we started getting back on our feet. We then heard that a local hairdressing salon was up for rent, and we decided to take it. I thought, 'We're getting £300-£400 for three days. We could be in the shop for six days and then we'll really be in the money.' We took a loan out and did it up with brand new chairs, sinks and everything.

We then sat down and waited for the customers, but no one came week after week after week. We'd done all the advertising and everything, but no one came. We had taken out a £5,000 loan and then we'd taken out another loan of about £5,000, and we had lots of other smaller loans. We got in a horrible state. Then Fran and I both lost our dads. By then Fran was only just starting to get back on good terms with her dad. After that, she just didn't want to go back to the shop, so I went up and stripped it all out and took the keys back to the landlord. That was it. It was 1996. We had about £20,000 debt at that stage, and had no income apart from income support, and I had incapacity benefit because of my asthma and diabetes. We then decided to go to the Citizens Advice Bureau in Tamworth for some help. They put everything down on paper and helped negotiate lower repayments for us and, for a while, everything seemed relatively under control. Unfortunately things started to build up again and I started thinking, 'What's going to happen to us? How are we going to continue like this?'

Then one day at the beginning of 2001, Ben (Fran's 16-year-old son) said, 'Guess where I've been today? I've been to church.' He had been taken by Fran's brother, Chris, and his wife, Helen. They were Christians and Ben had a part-time job working for Chris.

'Did you enjoy it?' we said.

'Yeah. It was really nice,' he said. That shocked us.

I said, 'Are you going to go again?'

He said, 'Yeah.'

After that, he started this thing called Alpha on Tuesday nights. Over the following months, we saw a massive change in Ben. Up until then he was pretty half-soaked – laid back and not very helpful – but that all changed. He was totally different – better. Fran and I started talking about him, 'Ben's totally different – isn't he? His attitude's totally changed.'

Fran said, 'I asked Ben the other day, "Ain't you

worrying about your exams, Ben?" And he said, "No, not at all." So I said, "Why?" And he said, "Well, the big man upstairs has got his hand on my shoulder." '

We thought that was lovely. That started us getting quite curious about church, especially as Ben was changing so much. It was as if he had matured and he was so calm. Before he started going to church, my relationship with Ben wasn't good at all. We clashed all the time, but bit by bit that all seemed to go. All the backchat just seemed to fall away. He didn't really say much to me about the Alpha course. Fran said to me one night, 'Do you know Ben's started this Alpha course thing?'

I said, 'No. What's that?'

She said, 'Oh, it's a course getting to know God and Jesus and readings in the Bible.'

I said, 'Oh, right.'

I wasn't really worried because I thought that if something like that could help him, and help him change so much, it had to be a good thing whatever it was.

Fran then said, 'Oh, I would like to do the Alpha course.'

I said, 'Well, there's nothing stopping you from doing it if you want to, but don't expect me to do it. I'll take you down there if you want.'

We continued to talk about the Alpha course over the following months. We were also talking about our life and what on earth we were going to do about it. Then we had a flyer come through the door from this organisation called CAP (Christians Against Poverty), that offered debt counselling. I didn't register the Christian side of it at all, but the word 'poverty' really stuck in my head hard, and I thought, 'I must try them, see what they're like.' We phoned them up and told them we'd seen the flyer and said we wanted to see them. This was around November 2001. The two ladies called Sue and Sylvia from CAP visited us. We all sat round the kitchen table and they made us feel so at ease. Once they'd gone through all our bills, they said, 'Would you mind if we said a prayer?' I was shocked. I didn't really know what to think. I looked at Fran and then said, 'Um, OK, go ahead, we don't mind.' She then said a prayer asking God for guidance with our finances, and asking him to help them help us. I thought it was lovely. A few days later they came up with some paperwork and afterwards we started talking about Christianity. We mentioned that Ben had started going to church and mentioned the Alpha thing and everything.

Sue then said, 'What about if I invite you to come to our church at Tamworth?'

We said, 'Umm, yeah, we'd love to come down.'

They had an Alpha course running at the time, and so we went down the following Tuesday, which was the night of the course. When we got there we walked in, and there were tables all laid out lovely. There were about eight tables set up with around six seats at each one – all in a church. It was quite surprising. We were welcomed to a table and sat down. I looked at the woman next to me and she said, 'Oh, hello Eugene.' It was the optician. Then on the other side of the table I noticed the lady from the library, and then all night I kept meeting people I knew. There were about 30-40 people there. We didn't know what the course really was. Ben had mentioned a meal, but we didn't really know what to expect.

After supper, the minister, Ian Bunce, gave a talk with quotes from the Bible. He broke it all down so well. I can't remember what the topic was that first evening, but it felt like he was talking directly to Fran and me about our life. I was nearly in tears. Then we had a cup of tea and a chat at each of our tables. The other people on our table were very nice. I liked the discussions, although the first week we just sat and listened. We didn't contribute much, we were just so curious. At the end, I left buzzing. I was absolutely battery-charged. We felt so lifted – there was no other way of describing it. We were just looking forward to the next one and wanted to go to church on the Sunday. Over the following weeks we continued to attend the course, and every Alpha evening we found the talks spoke so directly to us. We would both turn round and say, 'How strange, did you hear what he was saying? We were talking about that last night.' It was like he almost knew what was going on in our heads and in our lives.

Then, about three-quarters of the way through Alpha, we were in church when Ian said, 'If anyone would like God to come into their lives, then come forward and we'll get some people to pray for you.' I felt a hand gently pushing me forward but there was no one behind me. When I got up the front some people gathered round me and prayed for me. As they did so my whole life flashed before me and I started streaming with tears. The more they prayed, the more upset I got. The tears were for all the hurt I had inflicted on other people. It seemed to all come in front of me, and I asked God for forgiveness for it all. Then it was like a hand went down inside of me and took all the nastiness away. I then felt so elated – and that's how I've felt ever since.

After that service one of the people, Geoff, gave me a Bible, and Fran and I started reading it at night and we would talk about it all the time. At the Alpha Day Away, Ian started talking about letting the Holy Spirit into your life, and some of the helpers came round to pray for people. I thought it was lovely. I found it very relaxing. We finished the Alpha course in December, and we didn't know what we were going to do on Tuesday nights. We had made such good friends with our group. They were such nice people – people who worry about you, people who care for you. I had to have a double heart bypass not long ago and they all came to visit me. We had the nicest Christmas we've ever had. We went to church on Christmas day at Tamworth Baptist Church, and it was just lovely to be celebrating what Christmas is all about. Since then we've been doing a course in preparation for our baptism. We're about half way through.

Jesus has made a great difference in my life. I was an awful mess. He's brought me back to reality. It's wonderful. He's done wonders for us. We cannot get enough. We are still in debt but it's being resolved. We are so easy with it now. Sue negotiated on our part for one of the loan companies to cancel £7,000 of our debt if we pay £2,000 in £163 per month instalments, which is amazing.

We talk about God all the time and read our Bible. A friend came round the other day and we were talking about God for three hours. Fran and I also pray together, which is wonderful. I feel really sorry for my past. I really do feel sorry. I've hurt people, I've left people behind. But now I feel I've faced up to it and asked God to forgive me. The Alpha course gave me the means to get to know God. I still have problems, but they're not problems that do my head in anymore. They're just the normal problems of life. Our faith helps us to deal with things on an even keel now. When we're in trouble we just turn to the Bible or say a prayer together, and it really works.

Recently we had one or two hiccups and I was really angry and Fran said, 'Let's pray.' We just sat there and held hands and prayed. All the anger and uptightness just went away and I felt easy all day. That's how life is now. I never had an understanding about life really – not like I'm getting now from reading the Bible and from God being inside me. I love church as well. You're not just a number in a seat, you're made to feel important. The fellowship at our church is amazing – it's wonderful. It's like a new thing that's happening to us. It's glorious.

'I know where I'm going now . . .'

Fran's story

The night Eugene and I left, my children were all in bed. It's difficult to put into words how I felt that evening. I think I just blanked everything out. It was like that for a couple of weeks, maybe even a couple of months. You just blank everything. You have to, otherwise you wouldn't cope with it – especially the children side of it. After I divorced Karl, Eugene and I started to build our life together. However both our dads then died, and we then had this disaster with the hair salon and found ourselves in serious debt.

Towards the end of 2000, my mum started going to church with my brother, Chris – to Streetly Evangelical Church in Birmingham. I think after my dad died she thought, 'I need something to do, somewhere to go.' She then went on to do the Alpha course that October. She was the first person to mention it to me and she gave me the Alpha newspaper to read. She said how much she enjoyed it and kept saying to me, 'Just try it and see.' I would say, 'Yeah, OK mum, I will.' I could see a difference in her. She was calmer and coping better with life. My sister, Anne, then started an Alpha course at St Nicholas Church in Wrentham, Suffolk. It's a Church of England church. That was in May 2001. She phoned me up to tell me about it all and I sensed a change in her – she was very excited. Her husband Steve then did the next Alpha course after her and he also became a Christian. He didn't really have any belief before he did the course. They've got two young children – Emily and Thomas. The whole family got baptised.

Around that time Ben went to church with his uncle, Chris. I was very proud of him, because I knew that it would mean a lot to Chris. Ben then started doing the Alpha course at Chris's church. My mother helped in the group as well. It was quite difficult talking to Ben about it all, because I think he was a bit uncertain whether we were really interested in hearing about it. It would take a bit of time to get him to open up about it all. He was always quite excited when he came in from church, but then I would have to sit quietly with him for a while, to get him to talk about his feelings and what it was doing for him. Ben and I would then often have quite a deep conversation about what it meant to him. The more I heard from him the more curious I got. He would also talk about saying his prayers – that he would ask God to help him through his exams. Little things like that that kept on making me more and more interested. When Ben came back from the Alpha evenings he was always just so excited and buzzing with it. My brother would bring him back, and they would be coming in through the door going jabber, jabber, jabber, telling me what they'd been doing and everything. Then I started to think, 'If Ben can get this much out of it all, then there has got to be more to Christianity.'

Eugene and I then ended up seeing these people from CAP (Christians Against Poverty), who invited us to Alpha at their church, Tamworth Baptist Church. My first impression of the Alpha evening was of friendliness. I couldn't believe so many people could be so friendly. And this might sound funny, but it was great to spend an evening out of the house, because we hadn't been out much because of our money problems. The course gave me a lot more confidence, which I found building up over the weeks as I went.

Towards the end of the course, Ian, the minister, asked everyone to close their eyes and, if they wanted to, to follow him in a prayer of commitment to God – which is just repenting of your sins and asking Jesus into your life. I said the prayer. Afterwards Ian said, 'Keep your eyes closed. Anyone who said the prayer in their heart just raise a hand so I know you've said it, and I can have a word with you.' That was great because I quickly took the opportunity to raise my hand while no one was looking. I was very happy when I said the prayer. When we went to church on the Sunday Ian came up to me and gave me a little book for new Christians. He said, 'This is for you because you made a commitment the other night at Alpha.' That was great. It was like a sort of confirmation that I had made that commitment.

Since then the whole thing has given me direction in my life, because I know where I'm going now and I know who I'm following. It has put love back into my life and made me think about everything I do with a different – kinder – attitude. It's what I've been missing in my life. Now I know Jesus loves me. I do worry about what God thinks of the fact that both Eugene and I have both been married before. I have asked God for forgiveness for everything, but it still plays on my mind a bit.

Since Eugene's become a Christian he is a lot more tolerant of other people. He's got a lot more patience and he does a lot more thinking. Now he thinks first, acts after. Before he would act first, think after. There is a calmness in him and a strength – an inner strength and sense of peace. It's definitely strengthened our marriage. With regards to our debt, there's a light at the end of the tunnel. And we know that Jesus is there with us.

Eugene and Fran Ford continue to worship at Tamworth Baptist Church where they were baptised in June 2002. Fran's mother and sister were baptised in February 2003. Fran's son, Ben Price, is also a regular member of the church, where he says his faith 'continues to grow'.

8

'I was so confused.'

The story of Sarah Mansbridge

For 10 years Sarah Mansbridge of Wickford, Essex, was a Mormon. She was converted at the age of 19 when two smartly-dressed American men came to her door and asked if she would like spiritual guidance. Over the years, she rose in the Mormon church to being a member of the church's temple in Surrey. She had started to query her faith when some friends invited her on to an Alpha course. Here she tells the story of how her life has been transformed by Jesus Christ:

I wasn't brought up in a Christian family. My mum and dad have never been into any religion at all. They're just average I suppose. I left home when I was 17 and moved into a flat with my fiancé, Lee, when I was 18. We got married a year later. I got a job as a Care Officer at a Catholic-run charity, looking after adults with learning disabilities. Just before we married, I answered a knock on the door to find two smartly-dressed men in dark suits. They were American, young, very polite and were riding bicycles. They said, 'We'd like to talk to you about God and Jesus' and I thought, 'Oh, OK.' Lee was upstairs telling me to shoo them away, but I was interested and I let them in. They didn't stay for long, but they arranged to come and visit me at a later date. I liked them. They were nice and very interested in me. They came every week. On their visits they would get out pictures of Jesus and pick verses out of the Bible. Then they introduced me to something called the *Book of Mormon* which seemed to be their main emphasis.

Lee wasn't very happy about it but I wanted to believe in something, and they were telling me all this stuff and it seemed to be making sense. They said they were the only true church and all the rest of the Christian churches were wrong. I just followed along and, after about six months, decided to join the Mormon church. I thought, 'This is it. What they are saying is right.' One problem was that I couldn't join the Mormons until I married. I was so keen to join the church that we got married very quickly. Lee didn't believe any of it but he was happy to get married, so we had a very low-key affair in a registry office. Soon after that, I was baptised into the church. Lee came, but I didn't tell my parents because I knew they'd be shocked. Eventually I did tell them and they were shocked. They tried to convince me to come out of it, but I didn't want to listen to anybody because I knew it was right. That was it. I believed it was right and went along with it.

It is important in the Mormons to follow the rules so that

you are worthy to move up to their 'next level'. You had to
'pay your tithing, go to church every week and be worthy.'
The tithing meant that I had to give ten per cent of my earn-
ings to the church. The Sunday church service lasted for
three hours – from ten o'clock until one o'clock. The church
was about four or five miles from my home, and I used to
spend most of Sunday there. There would be a main meeting called a Sacrament meeting (where they used bread and
water), and then after that they'd have like an adult Sunday
school, followed by separate meetings for men and women
that I'd have to go to. During this time there were separate
meetings for the children as well. About a 100 people
maximum used to go (numbers would go up and down
depending on the time of year and the missionary efforts to
get people in). You weren't allowed to wear trousers if you
were a woman. You had to wear a long skirt and be in your
Sunday best. They were very strict about what you were
allowed to do and weren't allowed to do on Sundays. I
wasn't allowed to do any housework on a Sunday, and my
main focus was doing things for the church all the time. That
came first and everything else came after that.

We were taught that a man called Joseph Smith, who
lived in America at the beginning of the 19th century, was a
prophet who restored the true church to the earth after the
original church had fallen into apostasy. He taught that the
Father, Son and Holy Spirit are three separate gods – not one
God. Since then, there have been a succession of living
prophets on the earth, and the current one is called Gordon
B. Hinckley, who is president of the church based in Utah.

My husband was quite upset about all this. He didn't
believe any of it and it just caused tension between us. But
I was under a lot of pressure from the church to do things

that were required of me, so that I would be worthy enough. You are not allowed to drink tea, coffee or alcohol, and you are not allowed to smoke or do any sort of drugs. That was completely out. There were also lots of things I was expected to do on week days, like preparing lessons for teaching the children on the Sunday and going out visiting people. We were each assigned to visit different people within our congregation, and we were supposed to spend some time with them and read out of our magazines. All the women have to go and visit different 'sisters'.

I had been a member for five years when the bishop (who is like the equivalent of a minister in the Mormon church) told me he wanted me to go to the 'temple', which is the next level up. During this time in the church I was very busy and we had two children as well – Hannah in 1994 and Ben in 1997. There are two temples in the UK – one in Surrey and the other in Preston. Only a very small minority of Mormons get to go there because you have to be at the right standard of worthiness. You have to go to all your meetings and pay your tithing. Before going to the temple I had to go for an interview where I was questioned about all my beliefs, and also about a whole lot of personal information, to find out if I was good enough to go. You had to declare that you felt you were good enough to go to what was considered to be God's house. You had to say that you were worthy. I was always uncomfortable saying that I was worthy of anything, so that was a bit intimidating.

So I went to the temple (which is in Lingfield, Surrey), and when you go there everything is all secret. You're put under a lot more pressure because you go to these ceremonies and you're not allowed to talk about them. I went for a special endowment ceremony at which you have to wear special underwear, which is supposed to be a protection to you. After the ceremony you have to wear it all the time. It is called a sacred garment and is like long underwear right down to your knees, covering your arms and everything. I believed I had to wear it all the time – even when sleeping – to be protected. You didn't have to wear it when having a bath or going swimming or anything, but immediately afterwards you had to put it straight back on. It was horrible in the summer because it was like having thermal underwear on. I couldn't wear shorts or anything like that.

It was quite a long drive to the temple. Some people go once a month, some people go every week – it's down to you. Usually people go on Saturdays or during the week – sometimes all through the night. Then to church on Sundays – people do not attend the temple on Sundays. In the temple they do ceremonies which are connected to a lot of Masonic stuff. You have to learn the passwords, secret handshakes – everything you need to know to get into heaven. They do baptisms for the dead in there as well. So if anyone in your family has died and they weren't Mormons, you could be baptised on their behalf. You have to research your family history and get your ancestors' names and submit them to the temple, so that they can have their baptisms and all their other ceremonies done for them, so that if they're not Mormon in this life they become a Mormon after.

I was under quite a lot of pressure to get my husband into it as well, because they also believe that you have to be married in the temple. That is a special marriage that lasts in heaven as well. If you don't have that marriage you don't get to the highest level of heaven. I felt all this pressure because I knew I hadn't been married in the temple. I was quite upset, because I couldn't understand why God would say that I wasn't worthy enough to be in the highest level of heaven because my husband didn't accept it. My full salvation could not be achieved on my own. I would have to be married in the temple to a faithful Mormon to qualify to enter the highest level of heaven in the 'celestial kingdom' and be exalted. Only in the 'celestial kingdom' can you be in the presence of God. And if exalted, become like God. I couldn't understand some of the things I was being taught and it was a real conflict within me. To move to the next level would mean I would be exalted and have eternal life, they told me.

A little while after all this a couple of friends who were Mormons looked on the internet and found out information that had been hidden from them about the church – and it was very alarming. They found out that Joseph Smith, who was the prophet who founded the church, had had prophesies that hadn't come true. They also found out that parts of the *Book of Mormon* had been taken straight out of the King James Bible, which was strange as it was supposed to have been translated by the power of God from 'reformed Egyptian hieroglyphics' engraved on these gold plates that Joseph Smith had found. Also over the years many changes had been made and covered up. About 4,000 in the *Book of Mormon*. They also found out about many contradictions and changes in the teachings of the Mormon prophets which had been hidden, such as: man could become a god and each could have his own planet and people would worship him as their god. The second Mormon prophet, Brigham Young, taught that Adam was God – a teaching which is now rejected by the Mormon church. We were like, 'Oh, no. Is this true? Did they teach that?'

All this was coming from sources who had originally

been within the church and who, although they knew it was true, had actually denied it and hidden it and covered it up. They found out that Mormon prophets had taught that Jesus was married to more than one wife and had had children – which was another teaching that they don't openly teach and have hidden from most of their members. When I found out all this stuff, everything that I thought was true was turned upside down. I was left in this state of, 'Well, if this isn't true, there can't be anything else that is true.' That was in early 1999 (March).

My friends, Abigail and Paul, became Christians. Everybody else in the church didn't want to know them and wouldn't stay in contact with them. But I carried on being friends with Abigail and, despite my confusion, I was always trying to convert her back to being a Mormon. But the more she told me about the Mormon church which I didn't know, the more unsure I became. Meanwhile I was being told by the Mormons that if I left I was going to go to hell. From this time on I didn't know who was right and who was wrong, and couldn't make sense of anything. I was thinking, 'Well that's it. I might as well give up. Whatever I do I'm going to go to hell, so I might as well just give up now. I've had enough.' I was very depressed.

During this time – between March 1999 and August 2000 – I just backed off from everything. I was under too much pressure. I couldn't cope with it. I kept going along to the church on Sundays every now and then, but otherwise I stayed away. I was scared of leaving altogether because they say you're going to go to hell if you leave. That was really scary to me. I bottled it all up because I knew that if I told my husband he would insist I leave the Mormons. I couldn't talk to anybody in the Mormon church either because that would have got me into more trouble. All my friends were Mormons. I was just so depressed that I wanted to die. The thought crossed my mind a few times, but I wouldn't go that far. I just wanted to sleep. I thought it would be good to be dead and free of the constant torment and anguish. It was on my mind all the time and I became very withdrawn from everyone, including my family. I felt the only person I could trust was God, even though I didn't know who he was. I used to pray but I became confused about whether it was the right God or not. I just didn't know who I was praying to.

At around this time, some Jehovah's Witnesses came to my door and I started attending some of their meetings as well. They began coming to my house nearly every week to give me Bible studies. I started to think that if the Mormons weren't right, perhaps the Jehovah's Witnesses had it. But they had some different teachings altogether. With them you can't celebrate Christmas, Easter or birthdays. And you can't accept blood transfusions. I just got more and more confused. That was when my friends invited me on an Alpha course. They said it was a course to learn about Christianity and that there wasn't any pressure on it – you could just make up your own mind. I ummed and ahhed about it, and for a while I went back to the Mormons and cut off all contact with my Christian friends. I got rid of all the books that were against the Mormons and went back to try to be a really good Mormon again. All my friends there were pleased and said, 'Oh, isn't Sarah doing well? She's back with us again now.'

Then the bishop came up to me and said, 'Are you going to come back to the temple?'

Then I started to think about all the stuff I'd found out about the temple. I knew there was no way I could go back there. I knew it was wrong. I was kidding myself. I couldn't go back there. I just knew then that I couldn't do that.

The Alpha course was coming up again so I agreed to go on Alpha. I started the Alpha course in September 2000 – but even while I was attending the course, I was going to the Mormon church on Sundays. The Alpha course was held in someone's home. There were only about six or seven of us there and we watched the video. Throughout that first session I was very defensive and tried my best to prove that the Mormons were right. The second week I went along and had the same sort of attitude. Then on the third week Nicky Gumbel [the Alpha course speaker] read out a prayer where we could invite God into our lives. I had said prayers like that before but I'd never really meant it. But this time I said it, I meant what I was saying.

Following his lead, I said thank you for Jesus and that he had died for me. I asked God to forgive me for everything that I had done wrong in my life, and asked him to show me what was true so that I would really know. I said that I was putting all my trust in him and wanted the Holy Spirit to come into my life. I said these things really quietly, but as I said them, I knew that God was there. I really felt that I was talking to him. There was a presence there. I felt a reassurance, a calm, a peace and a love come over me. All the fear and confusion that I had just went. I knew that he was there and that he loved me and had forgiven me. This feeling of joy came up within me and all the relief of the pressure being lifted off me. It was overwhelming. I just knew then that Jesus had forgiven me. I was so happy. I went home with my friends and they were looking at me saying, 'Are you all right then?' I said that something really amazing had just happened and I felt wonderful. When I got home Lee wondered what was going on. I was walking around with a big grin on my face and was all bubbly and happy. It was such a change from the miserable, withdrawn person he had become used to. I think he wondered what was going on.

When I got back to Alpha the following week, I just sat there with a smile on my face. Then I told them how my life had been completely changed the previous week and how the pressure had been taken off. They all saw the change in me. After that I loved the Alpha course. We had an Alpha Day Away and I felt very close to God on that day. I am now attending church services at the Salvation Army in Wickford. The children come too and they love it. There is such a difference from what they've experienced at the Mormon church. My son loves being noisy, so when I was in the Mormons I spent most of the time in the corridor with him, telling him that he had to be very quiet. Now he can sing and be happy in church, which he loves. Now I know that I've got Jesus with me and he gives me the strength. I'm not working for a place in heaven like I was before. I know that I've got a place there and he loves me and he's forgiven me. It's not through anything I've done or worked for, but because he loves me and died for me. That means I've got no fear.

As a Mormon, I was taught to pray with lots of 'thees' and 'thous'. I had to think very carefully about what I was saying. Now I just talk to Jesus. Now I can read the Bible and understand what it is saying. It has become a new book to me. I was learning so much from it and I hadn't been able to see it before. I'd read the same passages before as a Mormon, except it was a completely contorted meaning and it hadn't made sense. Now I feel God speaking to me through the Bible and I have become so excited about it. It's amazing. Now I help on a daytime Alpha course with about eight or nine people on it and a crèche for the children.

I've sent a letter of resignation to the Mormon church asking them to remove my name from their records. At the end of my letter I told them that coming to know Jesus Christ as my Lord and Saviour had been the greatest thing that had ever happened in my life. I said that I believe that through Jesus Christ I have eternal life – and not through anything I have done or worked for. I feel that God has been gradually showing me the right way to go. I had to get to that point of trusting him and it took me 18 months to pluck up enough courage to do it. Now Jesus means everything to me. My life has changed completely because I was always trying to be good enough to earn a place in heaven, and now I realise that Jesus has made it all possible.

In early 2002, Sarah Mansbridge officially left the Mormon church and joined the Salvation Army, where she has been involved with several Alpha courses. She is also part of the local group of 'Reachout Trust', a Christian ministry helping people involved in cults.

'I called myself a witch.'

The story of Michael & Cathy Brunton-Spall

Michael Brunton-Spall, of Hull, was fascinated by the occult and called himself a Wiccan. For six to eight hours each evening, he would talk to people in chat rooms about his beliefs – often trying to help them with their problems. Then he wandered past a church which had a poster about the Alpha course in its window ... Here he and Cathy tell the story of how they went on a course and how their lives have changed since:

Michael's story

My parents got divorced when I was five or six. I remember lots of arguments. After the divorce neither of my parents particularly wanted to have me around. That was quite difficult. My mother met another man when I was about seven and he was very unpleasant. He always seemed to be tormenting me and putting me down. Throughout the whole of senior school I was very unhappy and got bullied regularly. I would bottle it all up and every now and then I would snap. I used to get really angry. When I was 17 I started working at McDonald's doing 11 to 12 hour shifts, six days a week. When I came home from work at 3am I couldn't sleep, so I started chatting on the internet every night for six to eight hours.

I got interested in all sorts of occult societies, particularly Theosophy and Wiccanism – witchcraft. I was bored by the big four religions and wanted to find out about fringe religions. I believed that much of it was psychological trickery, which is why I thought 'confidence spells' – to give people confidence – worked. If a friend asked me to say a confidence spell over them, I would try to make up a four line spell in the form of a song or poem – something along the lines of, 'We conjure Spirits of the air to watch over you in your job interview . . .'

They would come back later and say, 'That spell of yours really worked. I was really confident in my interview.'

I used to do tarot cards an awful lot and got very good at it. Friends would come to me for readings. I would lead them along, saying, 'You have a friend, probably quite tall . . .' and they would say, 'Yes, yes . . .' But my readings became more and more accurate – sometimes scarily accurate – so I stopped. I then got very interested in Anton Levay, the founder of the official religion of Satanism.

In the end I began to think of myself as a Wiccan. Wiccans do not believe that God is an outside being, but that the god or goddess is all of us on the earth. The main reason I called myself a Wiccan was that it is philosophically very easy-going. Wiccans could do anything – have sex, drink a lot and have as much fun as they liked, so long as they didn't hurt anyone. I thought, 'That sounds nice. I can go out and do whatever I want.' I called myself a witch which gave people an impression of me which I liked. They would be interested in me, whereas before I would be just a nobody. I started at Lincoln University in 1999, studying computer games design, and told my flatmates in my first term, 'I'm a Wiccan – but I'm not big on religion.' My ex-girlfriend called me a 'Fair-weather Wiccan'. I was more talk and less action – I loved to talk about the occult and that sort of thing, but it didn't really affect my life.

I met Cathy at a university drama society in October 2001 – my third year – and we started going out. She had been a Christian before coming to university but was going through lots of issues with her faith. She never wanted to discuss it though. Cathy and I started sleeping together and going out and drinking and all sorts . . . In around March 2002 she decided she wanted to go to church, to one called 'New Life' in Hull. I went about three times. I was a bit uncomfortable with the whole thing, but I knew I wanted Cathy to sort it out because she was falling to pieces really. She was becoming more and more depressed. She'd reached the point where she thought, 'I need God in my life – I can't run away from him any longer . . .'

I knew that something was happening in Cathy's life and I couldn't understand it. It was like, 'How do you compete with God?' It's not really a fair playing-ground. I e-mailed a Christian friend from Cathy's church in Royston, and she ended up sending me a Bible. I then read the gospels – Matthew, Mark, Luke and John. Then I had a period of one or two weeks where it felt like every time I looked around, there was something about God . . . I kept seeing posters around Hull with a psalm or a Bible verse. Then I got a little note through the door from one of the local churches about a student Bible study group. I decided to go along and find out what it was about. There was this Chinese guy and girl and me and Cathy. They were talking about how as a student you can look at the Bible to help you in situations and I was thinking, 'I didn't realise you could do that!' They were so nice and it was exactly what I needed.

Then I wandered past a church called Hull Community Church. They had a poster up in the window advertising an Alpha course. I didn't know much about Alpha, but Cathy had mentioned it a couple of times. By now I was working as a computer programmer for a company – but Cathy was still at university. She had been two years behind me. I started thinking of going on an Alpha course and told Cathy. She was pleased and said she thought I would enjoy it. So I phoned up Hull Community Church and went along to their course, which started in September 2002. Cathy came along with me to the course because I was bit unsure what it was going to be like. It was held in a small study room of the church and there were only about ten people there. We had missed the first week, but had a meal and sat down to watch the video on 'Who is Jesus?'

I loved the first week of Alpha – it was a forum that encouraged intellectual discussion. One of the guys who was there – Steve – had been through quite a lot. He'd have question after question after question. The guy leading it, Alistair – a really nice guy – would listen and then say, 'Does anyone else have a view?'

I'd say, 'I'm not a Christian, I don't believe in God.'

Then, because Steve kept asking all these questions, I'd sometimes say, 'Well, that's wrong...' And I'd end up arguing for the Christian side. I'd say, 'If God existed wouldn't it be like this, this and this . . .'

For the Day Away, we went to a Catholic retreat in Hornsea – a little seaside place. We had a ministry and prayer time and we got prayed for as a couple by Debbie and

Alistair, which was really nice. I didn't really feel anything more than I already had.

Some time after that, we had a guy called Simon come to speak on the course about being sure of your faith. And that was the most encouraging thing on the whole course. Because he said it had taken him about seven years to move from the time when he'd first started thinking about becoming a Christian, to being filled with the Spirit and having absolute faith that he was a Christian and believed in God.

At the end of Alpha they asked me, 'Would you consider yourself a Christian now?'

I said, 'No, not really – but I'm still interested and investigating . . .' So they invited us to come along to a home group.

It was a gradual process for me and the Alpha course was definitely the start of it. After Alpha finished we started going to the home group and the atmosphere was so friendly. We were still sleeping together – but the group never said anything. They were really accepting of us as we were. It was the perfect environment for us. And so in that accepting, loving environment I found my interest in Christianity was growing. After a few weeks I started meeting up individually with Simon to talk through issues or questions that I had. Cathy was also meeting up with Simon's wife, Sue, quite regularly to talk with her about her problems. It was the support, the family, the love that kept us coming back to the home group every week. In March I felt, 'Enough's enough – just get on with it.' So I decided to make a commitment to God. Cathy couldn't make home group that evening because she was nannying – and I was quite glad she wasn't there because I wanted it to be my decision alone. So I told Simon privately at the beginning of the evening, 'I'd like to pray a prayer and really dedicate my life to God.'

At the end of the evening I said, 'I just want to give my life to the Lord . . .'

And everyone went, 'Oooohhh!'

I basically prayed to thank God for being so patient with me, and to say publicly that I was going to give my life to him and that I was sorry that I'd made a mess of it already. I said, 'You can do a better job than me. I trust that you have plans for me and will do what's best for me.' And then lots of people prayed for me.

There were two things that really made me realise I was a Christian and that I had changed. Firstly, I really wanted to worship and praise God. One Sunday in church I realised that I'd sung along to every song – and I'd wanted to! I'd never done that before at all. That was a big change. The other big change was that we eventually stopped having sex. Cathy knew she didn't want us having sex any more, because she wanted us to get married and to do it properly, in God's sight. But she really wanted it to be my decision so that she'd know that God had spoken to me as well. Eventually I brought the subject up and said I felt we shouldn't be sleeping together. I knew it was the right thing to do. We went to see Simon and Sue and we talked about it and they prayed for us. Straight after they prayed we knew something had changed and that something had lifted off us. We thought the first couple of months would be really difficult but it was actually quite easy. God helped us through it.

In June 2003 we got engaged and we were married in November 2003. Cathy has noticed many changes in me. She says I'm still the Michael that she met, but she's seen the gifts of the Spirit growing in me. I used to have to be in control of everything because my life was so crap when I was younger, and the only way to deal with it was to be totally in control. Now it's like God has taken that and said, 'You don't have to be in control all the time . . .' And gradually I've learned to let go and let God be in control. And Cathy thinks I'm more relaxed in myself with who I am, because I don't have to come into every situation and control it.

We've been going to church regularly at Hull Community Church and are regular members of our care group, which is really good. My baptism was on 28 September 2003 – my birthday. It was a fantastic day, but I was really nervous. I was praying, 'I'm really nervous, I'm not sure I want to do this any more . . .'And suddenly it all drained away and I was like, 'Wow!' Now, if I get nervous about something, I pray and it goes.

'He's a different person.'

Cathy's story

I met Michael at drama class at university. He was in his third year and I was in my first. When I first saw him I thought, 'Ooh – he's a bit of a goth/weird type – black hair, beard, big black leather jacket . . . Not my type at all.' Then I started to get to know him and found that we had a lot in common. Something that attracted me to him was his spirituality and openness. I started staying over at his house and

at first everyone was making all sorts of comments. I'd
come to university as this good Christian girl and it was like,
'Scandal! She's staying over at a guy's house!'

When I first met Michael he was very interested in
Wicca. He told me it was part of the New Age movement –
part of paganism. He never went to church. He said, 'I agree
with some of their core things . . .' Basically it was like, 'Do
as you will, but harm no one.' or 'If you look out for number one you'll always be happy' – kind of thing. And don't
worry about God . . . He called himself a witch – but purely
because if you are part of the Wiccan faith and you give
other people advice, then you're a witch, you're sort of a
leader. He was often involved in chat forums where young
people would ask him for advice and he would give them
advice about magic and things like that. He met some of my
friends from my church at home and they knew he wasn't a
Christian. He was like, 'Oh they're all going to hate me
because I'm not a Christian . . .' And he deliberately tried to
be as sort of obnoxious and awful as he could to see what
reaction he'd get.

On the first night of Alpha I said to God, 'God, here I am
and I'm totally broken. I'm sorry for trying to run away
from you . . . How arrogant I've been to think that I could
get away from a God that's everywhere and a God that died
for me and loves me so much . . .' Then I sort of said, 'Well
God, what do I do about me and Michael? If you want us to
stop sleeping together you need to say it to Michael –
because I can't do it in my own strength and he can't do it
in his own strength.'

Michael loved the Alpha course but by the end he still
wasn't a Christian. It was like God was already working in
him and doing things, but he hadn't got to the point yet

where he was ready to say, 'Yeah – this is definitely it.' We started meeting individually with the two leaders of the home group and praying with them. And then in April Michael decided, 'Right – I'm really going to make a commitment.'

It was so exciting – and such a transformation happened. He seemed lighter as a person – more alive. It was amazing. You could see a physical difference. I don't know how to put it into words but he's a different person.

Now that we have Jesus involved in our lives, my relationship with Michael is amazing. It's like we can pray together and there's such a sense of unity in that. He's a constant encouragement. I feel like I can be totally relaxed about him now. I've always been very relaxed, but now it's like I can share all of my life with him. We're completely honest with each other. He's as passionate about Jesus as I am.

Michael and Cathy Brunton-Spall regularly attend Hull Community Church and help out on local Alpha courses.

9

'I led a pretty wild life. The university rugby club is a very non-Christian place to be.'

The story of Olly Arengo-Jones

Rugby player Olly Arengo-Jones was intrigued when he made friends with fellow students at Oxford Brookes University who he later learned were church-goers. As they developed into close friends, he began to question some of his own attitudes to life. Then they invited him on an Alpha course . . .

My mother is Catholic and used to take my elder brother, Tim, and me to church every Sunday. We used to hate getting up on Sunday mornings to go to church for the 10.30am service. My father was in the army working for NATO and so we lived in lots of places, including Berlin, Rome, Brussels, as well as the UK. Dad was Church of England but used to come with mum and us, but as we got older our churchgoing got a bit slacker and we'd go on Christmas and Easter. My mum was under a lot of stress at the time, following our move back to England, and was working hard.

I went to boarding school, which had a rule that if you were Catholic and had the written consent of your parents, you could attend a Catholic church instead of school chapel on Sundays. So my brother and I found a church, went a couple of times, and then realised this was a great thing because we could say we were going, walk out of the school, and then just walk straight back in the back door and sit around in our room and watch TV. If a master found us and asked us why we weren't at church, we would make some pathetic excuse. We continued going at Christmas because that just seemed the right thing to do. We were living in Richmond at the time and I remember one year my mum was ill and my dad was cooking the turkey, so Tim and I went to church by ourselves. I always thought it was rude if you didn't go to church at Christmas. I thought, 'We have this great big party and this fantastic time, it is only right that we should go.' So we went on our own and it was a very boring service – terribly dull.

After leaving school, I spent part of my gap year in the Caribbean doing various things. Then I worked in the Harrods toy department for six months and ended up staying with a friend called Toby in Florida. I never really thought about church throughout that time. Toby had a girlfriend in New York and we went to stay with her family. It turned out that her mother was a preacher at a local church – and it was an extraordinary place. There were crutches and zimmer frames and wheelchairs pinned around the walls of this massive church. The service wasn't that full, but there was lots of live music and I thought it was quite cool. I enjoyed the singing and the atmosphere and the girl's mother was very sweet, generous and nice to me.

In 1999, I went to Oxford Brookes University to study Economics and Accounting. When I arrived, church was the last thing on my mind. I played rugby for the university and led a pretty wild life. The university rugby club is definitely a very non-Christian place to be. You go out on Wednesday nights after the game and get absolutely wasted. The players go to a club in Cowley which is renowned (without being disrespectful) for having some women who are not exactly pure virgins, if you know what I mean. For most people at 'Brookes' it is the best club. And I thought it was great.

In fact, I was very happy with my life and could not complain at all. I had a great family, a really good bunch of mates and had no trouble meeting new people. My perception of Christians at the time was like a comedy sketch I saw where the Christians don't appear to have any muscles in their arms, but just walk around with their hands flopping around at their sides. But then I met a guy who was playing first rugby with me. I met him half way through the first term and got on with him very, very well. I thought he was a fantastic guy, and somehow I got to know that he was a Christian. Every Wednesday he'd finish a rugby match and just vanish and nobody would know where he was. He never came to the club on Wednesday nights until very late, when you would suddenly see him dancing. I later learned he was doing the Alpha course at Holy Trinity Brompton on Wednesday nights. He didn't drink a lot, but one thing I noticed was that when he did drink, he could down a pint so quickly it was unbelievable – two seconds or so…not bad! But then he would never drink anything else. He would never get drunk. I just thought, 'This guy has got different values to the rest of us.'

Then there was a girl at university called Katie Jennings – a fantastic girl – who was obviously very different to every other girl. She too, I learned, was a Christian. This guy I knew had a family house in Chelsea and he invited me to London one Sunday to go to church at Holy Trinity Brompton. A lot of people are always visiting London from Brookes because it's only 40 minutes by car at the most. So one Sunday night we went to church.

We went to the five o'clock service and I quite enjoyed it. The music was nice and the talk was good. I also met some of the church's student leaders, and I met one guy called Matt and we talked about rugby for ages. I'd learned that my friend had done this course called Alpha and I was quite interested. Then I started going out with Katie and I wasn't quite sure what I was getting into. I knew that we wouldn't be sleeping together or anything like that because of her Christianity, and I was outwardly quite happy with that, but I wondered where it would go a few months down the line. I thought to myself, 'How are you going to cope with this?' I've only had two or three relationships in my life that have been serious, and to start with I never wanted to sleep with them immediately. It didn't seem right with those kind of relationships. So that's what I felt with Katie and I was quite OK with it.

I read *Questions of Life* and I began to think more about Christianity. I had always believed there was a God and I never doubted that Jesus existed. Katie and I were going out from the summer of 1999, and I was a bit worried that if I did an Alpha course and became a more committed Christian, I would have been doing it for her. But I thought,

'Well, it's not going to work if I do it for her, is it? I've got to do it for me and my own faith.' I got on really well with Katie's family. I loved her mum and dad and I thought her two brothers, Piers and Tim, were the most fantastic people. They were all Christians and spoke constantly about their faith and miracles they had seen in their family. I just thought, 'These people aren't going to lie to me. They're not the sort of people who would lie.'

I read John's Gospel, which Katie said was the first one you should read. But when the September 1999 Alpha course came round, I thought, 'I'm not quite ready for this yet.' Around that time, my attitude to Wednesday nights with the rugby guys changed. It stopped being a case of going out and getting drunk because Katie wasn't into that and I was very happy to stop. She and I would go to the club, and I did get nosed a bit, but not as much as I did before. I still got drunk – I didn't have any problems with that – but probably not so often. One thing I did stop was the way I used to say 'O God' and 'Jesus Christ', in slang. Suddenly I wasn't quite so comfortable with it.

In the end I decided to do the April 2000 Alpha course. After months of putting it off, I said, 'Right, I'm going to do it' and I signed up. I had got to know Matt Costley and I was in the group he was leading on the course, so I felt very comfortable about it all. By the time I did the course, I had spent so much time with Katie and her family that I was already trying to be a different person – trying not to get drunk and not to be nasty to people the whole time. As the course went on, I got more and more agitated that nobody had told me this stuff about Jesus before. Why didn't anybody at school teach me that? Why didn't my RE teacher teach me that? At school they just seemed to teach the Bible as if it was an English text book, which frustrated me. When it came to the Alpha Weekend in Bath, I was a bit worried because Katie and I were due to go to her cousin Rachel's 21st birthday party on the Saturday night. Katie's brother Piers was also at the weekend and was also going to the party, which we had accepted ages before.

On the Saturday afternoon, my group leader Matt and another member of the group, Phil, prayed for me. As they prayed, I slowly started to cry – and then I found myself crying for ages. I just felt so sorry for all the things I had done wrong. All the time I was thanking God for all he had done for me – and every time I said 'thank you', I cried more. Every time I stopped crying I'd say 'thank you' again and start crying again. The only time I have ever cried like that was when my grandfather died at the end of my final school year. I knew him very well because my parents lived abroad and I saw my grandparents a lot. I thought to myself, 'Why am I crying?' – and I was getting the feeling I was just upset at the way I was and what I'd done. I wasn't doing drugs or anything like that, but my values were all wrong I think. I had no respect for women. I definitely felt that my views and my morals were not good. That was obvious to everyone who knew me – even those who were not Christians. We prayed for about half an hour and afterwards it was just amazing – genuine joy. It was the first time in my life I'd experienced such sheer joy.

We went to the birthday party that night, but came back for the rest of the weekend the following morning. There was another opportunity to receive the Holy Spirit then and I just lay down and Phil came up and prayed for me for ages. Suddenly I started giggling and every time I thanked God for it, I just started laughing even more. By the end of the weekend, I found I was thinking about God all the time. He was constantly on my mind. I wouldn't say that every action I've made since that weekend has been wholly Christian – I wouldn't say that at all – but every time I make a mistake the first thing I think about is God. I find myself saying, 'Sorry I did that' and I continually ask for forgiveness. I'm still nowhere near a perfect Christian, but I hope I'm making progress.

Before Alpha, I took all my decisions for myself, on the basis of what was going to be best for me. Now, when making a serious decision, I'd like to think that I'd pray about it. Over the summer months, I have read several books of the Bible including Acts, Romans, Hosea, Corinthians – and now I am half way through Jeremiah, which is the longest book I think I have ever read in my life! I am also reading a great book called *My Utmost For His Highest*, which I read every day. It is absolutely fantastic.

Jesus is now in me the whole time, and I make decisions based on my relationship with him and how I should be living my life from a Christian sense.

Olly Arengo-Jones married Katie Jennings on 1st December 2001 and they are now members of Holy Trinity Brompton, along with their son Benjamin, who was born in July 2003.

'My life was so empty – I began to feel "What's the point of it all?"'

When 20-year-old medical student Ben Loynes finished the Alpha course at the end of 2002, he wrote a moving letter to speaker Nicky Gumbel which was later published in Alpha News. Here Ben tells the full story of what happened to him on Alpha:

The story of Ben Loynes

I did the whole Sunday school thing with my family, but as a kid and a teenager I was a bit cynical about it. I stopped going to church after a while. My mum has always gone to church. My main objective in life was to get the highest grades I could at school. I became quite successful at that – got the A stars at GCSE and As at A-level and so on. But the more I achieved the more I expected of myself.

I've always wanted to be a doctor. My dad was ill with colitis when I was young and I was always visiting him in the hospital, where I would watch and admire the doctors. I got the A-level grades to get into Bart's & The London Medical School. Although it was a difficult adjustment it was exciting and my first year was quite mad really. I lived in a hall of residence with 12 blokes sharing two toilets and one shower – nasty. It was all student medics in this big tower block and was really scabby. At school, when I had been striving for academic success, I knew that if you took that away there wasn't much underneath. The thing I would fall back on was my family. But when you go away from home you begin to need something else in your life to hold on to. I found friends, but it wasn't enough for me. Something wasn't quite there. I began to feel, 'What's the point in it all?'

I had a few quite close Christian friends at university but I always avoided having conversations about God with them. At times I thought Christians were a bit arrogant. That summer (2002) I was sitting in our beach hut at Felixstowe discussing things with my mum. I said to her, 'My life's not right – it's not going in a good direction. I'm heading for a bit of a crash.' My main aim in life had always been achievement and I realised how empty it was.

I knew what my mum was going to say, 'Go find a church . . . Go to Christian Union . . . Find nice Christian people . . . and you'll be all right.'

I said, 'But I don't really believe it . . .' Then I said, 'OK, I'll look for a church, mum. And if that doesn't work I'm going to ditch it.'

So I started looking for churches in London on the internet. I came across the Alpha course – and found out that this church called Holy Trinity Brompton had started it. I hadn't heard of Alpha or Holy Trinity Brompton before, but it sounded as if the Alpha course would be a good way to investigate it all. The group thing sounded painful – sitting in a circle having discussions . . . Something I try to avoid. But I thought, 'I'll turn up for the ten weeks. If it's the last thing I do I'll definitely do that.'

It was the October 2002 course. I missed the first week because of the fireman's strike. The tubes weren't running and all the buses were completely packed. I was quite annoyed, but I turned up the second week. I was put into a group and my leader was a guy called Ben Homer. He was a lovely bloke – welcoming, funny, friendly – everything anyone would want to be really. He took me under his wing that first week – made a real effort to get to know me, which I thought was nice. The talk that night was, 'Why did Jesus die?' The talk was thought-provoking and I found it very persuasive. But I didn't say a word in any of the group discussions. In group situations, I freeze and clam up and don't say anything.

I wasn't really looking forward to going back because I'd found the group discussion so intimidating, but I forced myself to go to week three, week four . . . And each week I found myself being exposed to questions I hadn't asked myself. I'd never been a very philosophical person ('What's the meaning of life?' – I never went in for that). But now I began to think about these important questions. There were lots of lovely people in the group. They were all in their twenties, so a little bit older than me. After a couple of weeks I loved my group. After the group discussion we'd go to the pub, where I talked a bit more. I was more comfortable with trivial things like football. But I started debating seriously for the first time in my life whether God was there. Then came the Alpha weekend.

As a medical student, I've always got a lot of work and I thought I might use that as an excuse to avoid going on the weekend. I thought, 'I don't really want to waste my time.' But all the others were going (except one) and on the Friday of the weekend, Ben rang me and persuaded me to come. So I went – a bit grudgingly – and Jay, a helper in the group, gave me a lift. On the Saturday Nicky Gumbel [the Alpha course speaker] gave the talks on the Holy Spirit and speaking in tongues. I thought, 'How much more weird stuff do I have to believe?' – but I found the talks interesting and thought-provoking. Later that day I felt like I needed to speak to someone – and my mum was the obvious choice. It had been quite intense and I needed to get a bit of perspective. So I rang her up and said, 'I've never heard you speak about tongues – what's all this about?' She had heard of it and said she believed that people could speak in tongues and that I shouldn't worry. I wasn't really sure – so I just left it at that.

By the Sunday morning I just wanted to get home. After Nicky's talk he said a prayer for people who wanted to let God into their lives. At that moment it dawned on me that I had been defensive all weekend. I decided to drop my guard a bit and thought, 'I'll try and pray and open myself up to this.' So I let down the barriers and thought, 'This is the final chance – this is the end of the Alpha weekend. If nothing happens now, it never will.' I'd never really prayed like that before. I hadn't even prayed in times of crisis in my life. For the first time I asked God for forgiveness – which was kind of strange, because I'd never thought of myself needing forgiveness. I prayed, 'I want to believe in you, God. I want to live a Christian life, but I've never felt your presence. I know I've rejected you many times and I'm sorry for that, and I'm sorry for the things I've done that have hurt you. And I'd like now to be in a relationship with you.'

At that moment I began to feel something and I thought, 'Oh goodness!' I began to feel very out of control and started crying. I was sort of brushing away the tears, thinking, 'I can't cope with this.' I felt this sort of force filling me up – I can't describe it in terms of emotional words like 'happiness' or 'joy'. It was just this completely overpowering sensation. I knew it was God saying, 'I'm here.'

Someone in my group who wasn't a Christian later asked me, 'Were you crying because you were happy or sad?'

The way I'd describe it now is that it felt like this overwhelming love from God. I knew it wasn't something my imagination was conjuring up. It was too much for that. It was a completely unique emotion. I'm not very emotional so it was kind of a big thing for me. Before I knew it everyone was leaving the hall and I had to regain some sort of control. I started to walk, but then I thought, 'I just can't cope with this – this presence is still filling me up.' I felt like I couldn't walk out of the room, so I just collapsed into a chair. I started crying again and Jay came over and said, 'Jesus loves you, Ben, and he's trying pretty hard to tell you . . .' That is exactly what I felt – and it was nice for someone to translate it.

Ben prayed for me back in our room and I felt peace. Then Jay drove me home, tired but exhilarated. The following day I woke up and felt this love – a presence – and I could feel I was different. I got up and went for a walk. I live on Mile End Road – it's a really long road and I walked for ages, thinking about God and everything that had happened. For the first time in my life I was sure God was there. I felt so excited. It was a turning-point in my life. I knew from that day onwards life would be different. After walking I went back to my place and decided to write it all down – like a diary entry. Then I thought, 'I want someone to read this.' So I decided to send it to Nicky. Soon afterwards Nicky asked if he could read out bits of my letter in a sermon and I said yes. I was sitting with my sister in the church when he read the letter and she broke into tears (I hadn't told her it was going to happen). She was quite moved by the letter. I said, 'What did you think?'

And she said, 'Oh I thought that was really wonderful!'

Afterwards we walked along Oxford Street – quite unusual for me to be willing to go shopping – and we talked in a deep and meaningful way about God and my experience. That's the first time I'd ever spoken to my sister in that way. Her view was that, 'If Ben can experience that and break into tears it must be true.' Now she and a friend of mine from medical school are on the current Alpha course.

I finished Alpha a different person. It was as if my emotions had been opened up. I'd experienced God's love and it had changed me personally. Suddenly I had a desire to serve God and spend time in prayer. For weeks afterwards I'd wake up and lie in bed thinking, 'Oh, I feel really different. Why do I feel different?' And then I'd remember what had happened.

I'm still ambitious but now I'm driven not by my desire for success, but by what God wants me to do. I always wanted to be a doctor for good reasons – to help people – but there was still a part of me that thought becoming a doctor was going to be another achievement. Now the way I see my future medical career with Jesus in my life is quite different. I feel God's given me a greater ability to be a doctor. I've realised that he loves me and has blessed me with a greater ability to love other people.

Ben Loynes regularly attends Holy Trinity Brompton and has joined a student group in the church.

10

'I made a list of all the people I wanted to
be reconciled with.'

The story of Warren Kencroft

*Abandoned by both his parents at the age of four,
Warren Kencroft was brought up in a succession of
children's homes until the age of 12, when he moved in
with his father again. It was an upbringing which
made him, in his own words, 'emotionless'. Here he
describes how he worked hard to achieve a successful
career in management, but how his long hours took a
toll on his marriage. Then, in spring 2001, he was
invited on an Alpha course and his life began to
change:*

I have two brothers, one older, one younger, called Richard
and Mark. When I was four years old, our parents split up
and walked out on us, leaving us in the house on our own.

We woke up one day in our house in Greenford and they weren't there. I was four, Richard was five and Mark was just four (there was less than a year between us). We were in the house for a day and a half on our own. Mark was still in nappies and my elder brother was changing him. We just stayed in the house, too scared to go out, too scared to call anyone. Whenever the phone rang we didn't pick it up because we were so scared. Then someone came knocking on the door. My younger brother was the only one bold enough to go and see who it was. He stood on a stool and looked through the letterbox. It was a policeman. He stood there arguing with him, saying, 'I'm not letting you in because you are a stranger.'

The policeman eventually came in and the three of us were separated and put into temporary foster care. For the following two years, we saw very little of each other. We didn't have proper schooling at all – we just moved from place to place. I still don't know where my mum and dad went to. I just wanted them to get back together again, but it never happened. A year later, my dad got back in contact with us again and came to see us at our various homes. Mark remembers that he was very pleased to see us and said that he wouldn't leave us again – but I don't remember it. He was a minicab driver, but he didn't have a place where he could look after us. He had nowhere. He went on to a council housing waiting list, but nothing was to come up for another seven years.

When I was about seven, we started living in a series of children's homes. My dad started living in a bedsit with a lady called Gay (who was to become his wife), and we would visit them every fortnight on a Sunday. They would come and pick us up from the children's home. The first home was in Teddington and there were about five or ten of us children in it. I didn't like it at all and was always running away. The 'auntie and uncle' who ran the home made us stand in the garden in our shorts and T-shirts in the middle of winter to 'toughen us up'. They used to call us 'Big Jessies' if we cried. We would sit there shivering on the step waiting to come back in. I used to run away with a friend. I had memorised the trip to my dad's home near Ealing Broadway and we used to walk there. I would never go up to the door. We would just sit outside somewhere. We never stayed away more than a night. We would run out of food and then go to a police station and say we were runaways.

In all we probably lived in six or seven children's homes. I certainly went to five different schools, that I remember. It was not an easy time. One of our 'uncles' was later convicted as a child molester. When I was 12 my father was given a council house, and the three of us moved in with him and his partner, Gay. Gay was brilliant. She wasn't old, she hadn't had any previous marriages or relationships, and yet she was prepared to look after the three of us when we were not easy. She was our angel and very quickly became a surrogate mum to us. Our experiences in the children's homes had made us almost emotionless. We were hard to love and found it hard to love other people. We continued to stick closely together, and brother Richard was always looking out for us, just as he had been in the children's homes.

So we had a new home, a new school and everything was fresh – but unfortunately I think the past played on us and we were all very unruly. I got involved with the wrong crowd and used to be a hooligan breaking windows, smashing telephone boxes and shoplifting. I was very disruptive and cocky in class and found myself at rock bottom by the time I got to high school. But when I got there I had an English teacher called Mr Colerio, who gave me the attention that I needed. Up to that point we were left very much on our own. My dad and foster mum didn't come to school parents' evenings either. While other parents wanted to go and see how their children were getting on, mine just weren't interested. I'd give them the leaflet about it and leave it to them. I never told them I'd like them to come – we never talked about it.

Mr Colerio became like a father figure for me within a very short time. I looked up to him and he tried his best to push me through English and Maths. He gave me this confidence that I could do better. And he was right because I started moving up from class to class, until I had reached the top general graded class of the school. I went on to pass all of my GCSEs with straight grade As. At school I got involved in athletics and cross-country. I could beat almost everyone in the school at running. I won the Middlesex Schools and was in the National Schools Team for cross-country. Suddenly I became a bit of a recluse from my friends. I became a member of Thames Valley Harriers, and after leaving school would spend all my leisure time with them.

I got a job with London Underground and did a four-year engineering apprenticeship with them. Then I started working at their Cockfosters depot as a vehicle bodymaker, before moving into project management. I found I had a real knack for managing people and I was promoted quickly. I became a successful Senior Project Manager with London Underground Ltd. I have two loving boys from a failed marriage – Joshua, aged six, and Laurence, aged four. They have obviously become one of the main focuses in my life and are both doing extremely well – despite the break-up of my marriage.

Eventually I did meet my mum again. For 20 odd years she had never once sent a card, note, letter – and I had a terrible resentment towards her. In April 1996 my brother Mark organised for her to come to his house and I met her there. I was very, very cold towards her. There was no apology. I wanted to know that she was pleased to see me and that she was sorry she left us, but she acted as if nothing had happened. I was so annoyed, so upset. Over the next few months I went down to her place near Margate and found out she had a daughter, Lorna – my half sister – and that I had a grandmother and three aunts I didn't know about. It was just too much.

It was all going OK until Joshua's first birthday the following month in May 1996. My mum wanted to come, but my dad – who also wanted to come – had made it clear he wanted nothing to do with my mum. So I told her she couldn't come to the party, but she could come down another day. After that she wouldn't speak to me for about a week. I still persisted and went down the following Christmas. She refused to speak to me when she saw the photos from Joshua's party, so I left on a bad note and I have not seen her since.

During the latter part of 2000 I met a woman at work called Nicky, and we got chatting about life in general, and also about some of my problems/questions I had about life. During one of our chats she said to me, 'Why don't you come along to Alpha?'

I said, 'What's Alpha?'

She said it was a course where you could find answers to

some of these questions. She said, 'You'll meet some new friends.' I was quite lonely at the time, so I said yes.

It was held at her church, Holy Trinity Brompton. I found that first night quite scary as I had not expected it to be in such a big church. I sat there for the first few weeks looking for hard evidence for the existence of Jesus and God. I missed several weeks of the course in the middle, and the Alpha Weekend as well, because I went on holiday to South Africa. So the course didn't really work for me. I found it too fast. Week two was asking about the message of Jesus, and I had not even accepted who or what he was. I had never read the Bible or was familiar with the stories around the Bible. But at the end of the course I wanted to know more, I needed to know what it was all about. I wanted to come and do another course, but not before I knew a little more.

After that course Nicky bought me a Bible, which was superb, and I started going to church regularly at HTB. I thought the services were brilliant. I loved them from the start. The warmth and feeling of love when I entered the church was a marked contrast to that which I felt on the Alpha sessions. I signed up for the next Alpha course at the beginning of October, but missed the second and third session because I was running an 'extreme marathon' in the Kalahari. The race was 250 kilometres over seven days. You have to carry your week's supply of provisions. To train for it I had been getting up at 4am, and running from my home in Ruislip to my work in Canary Wharf, with a pack on my back. I sometimes did as much as 38–40 miles. There were only 13 runners in the race and I was the only person from England. I actually ended up winning, which was a complete surprise.

My second Alpha course was wonderful. Tom and Helen Adam were the group leaders and they were brilliant. My two boys came on the weekend, which was great. After the talk on the Holy Spirit, Tom prayed for me and I found myself shaking all over. It was like I had goose pimples up and down my arm. As he prayed, I asked for forgiveness for all my sins – everything I had done wrong in my life. It was a long list. I forgave people like my mum – everyone who had ever done anything to me. I cried my eyes out, but I wasn't embarrassed. I felt like it was the right thing to do. I actually said to God, 'I'm yours to use as your tool. Teach me your ways.' I remember saying, 'Tell me where you want me to go. Where should I be? What should I be doing?' The very next thing I did was grab my boys and give them a big hug and told them I loved them.

I made a list of all the people I wanted to reconcile with. It was a long list. One of the main people on the list was my mum. But there were also many people on my list who were from work, and who, as manager, I had 'encouraged to go and work elsewhere'. Basically I just wanted to say sorry to them. Shortly after Alpha I phoned my mum, and she was totally suspicious about my motives for calling. She thought I was after something. I forgave her for all she had said and done to me, and asked for forgiveness likewise for all I had done and said to her. She was very sceptical and slightly scathing, but I have not given up and we are at least now talking. I am hoping to see her soon when our forgiveness for each other has healed the wounds of the past. Many things in my past still hurt. There are things that happened in my life I can't just ignore. I do believe that all things are done for a reason. There is a reason why I went through that pain. I don't understand it, but I don't necessarily believe I have to understand it. When I became a Christian, it was as if all that pressure on my shoulders was just falling off and I was walking taller. I could feel myself bouncing along.

I now read the Bible every morning on the train to work. I don't care who sees me. I'm not embarrassed. My attitude to people has totally changed. I used to have what I called my 'three-strike rule'. If someone made one mistake, I'd let them off. If they made the same mistake a second time, I looked on it as stupidity. But if there was a third one, that was it. I wouldn't want to know them again. I used to treat everyone the same. I didn't have a huge list of friends. But when I read the Bible, I learned that there should be no level where you stop forgiving. I read the book, *What's So Amazing About Grace?* which I think is a fabulous, stimulating read.

I regularly thank God for bringing those people into my life like my close friend Nicky, my boss Jeff at work, and all the people I have met on the Alpha course who have been instrumental in my spiritual enlightenment in becoming a Christian. Becoming a Christian has changed my attitude to my mum and dad and everything I went through as a child.

I now have a daily relationship with God. I like to think I am a different person now – much more tolerant. Where there's an argument or an issue, I will try and be the first one to apologise and say I'm sorry. Now I know I have a purpose – I want to help others who are less fortunate than me.

Warren Kencroft remains a member of Holy Trinity Brompton. He now works part-time for the charity 'Grandma's' – which helps families and children whose lives have been affected by HIV. He says, 'It is extremely humbling work and it has helped me understand the true value of love – God's love. When I think back to where I was and how he has changed my life – staggering.'

'I couldn't help feeling that God had been with me all along, getting me freed from jail . . .'

The story of Deborah Field

In 1994, Deborah Field smuggled two kilos of 'grass' from Jamaica to Miami – and was caught when a dog sniffed her case as she was coming off the plane. It was the beginning of an experience which would culminate in her going on an Alpha course at her local mother-and-toddler group in Jersey. Here she tells how her newfound faith helped her through a terrible family tragedy . . .

I came to Jersey in around 1979 when my first marriage broke up. My mum and dad had moved to the island from London and I came to live with them. In 1994, I went on an extended holiday to Jamaica and used to play dominoes in a particular bar most nights. One night, I was about to go home when the barman, a friend called PeeWee, persuaded me to stay. He said, 'Just have one last drink.' About five minutes later a man walked into the bar and I thought, 'Oh, I like him.' His name was Wade and I got talking to him – and that was it. We saw each other every night after that.

I was very short of money and one day, after I'd been in Jamaica for about a year and a half, this chap came up to me and said, 'I know how you can make some money.'

I said, 'How?'

He said, 'Take these drugs over to America.' He held out some grass which they used over there. It's very common and most people use it. I'd never actually touched drugs before. I used to have a few drinks and that was all. So I said, 'No.' Then, after a while, it just got so desperate. I never told Wade that I didn't have any money – not even for food. I thought he'd got enough worries of his own. So in the end I said to the man, 'Yes, I will do it.' They asked me to take heroin or cocaine over, and I said no, because although the other stuff is illegal, it can't kill anybody. I refused point blank. They tried to persuade me with more money, but I said, 'No, I'm not interested. I don't care if I starve to death – I wouldn't do that.' So I did it one time (taking the grass) and everything went fine. Then they said to me, 'Do you want to do it again?'

I said, 'I'll do it one more time and then that will get me out of financial difficulty.'

I took the drugs – two kilos of grass – on the aeroplane concealed in the bottom of a holder. As I got off the plane in Miami, there was a dog there with some customs officers. Suddenly, as I passed, the dog got all excited. There were about six of us leaving the plane at the time, and we all had to put our luggage on the floor to allow the dog to sniff it. When the dog came to mine, he just sat down next to it. I was petrified because I had never been in trouble with the police before or anything. They took me to a room in the airport and started questioning me. When I went to the loo, there was always a police woman who came with me in case I had swallowed anything and it was going to come out. I was taken to jail and then to a courthouse where I was told that my case was going to be in three weeks time.

The following Sunday, there was a little chapel service in the prison and most of the people go to it. Although I had never been a churchgoer, I did believe in God and I went along. It was a very moving service because there was this girl there who was HIV positive and they prayed for her. After the service, a black girl came up to me and asked, 'Do you believe in God?' and I said that I did.

Then she said, 'Do you go to church?'

I said 'No.'

She said, 'Do you read the Bible?'

I said 'No.'

She said, 'You have got to start reading the Bible.'

I said, 'No, I'm not interested in that.'

But she hassled me relentlessly day in and day out and after about three or four days I said, 'All right, I'll read the Bible.'

At that, she gave me Psalm 23, which begins, 'The Lord is my Shepherd . . .' She said, 'Read it, read it all the time. Just keep reading it.'

Then she persuaded me to go along to a Bible study class, which was all about forgiveness. As it happened, one of my brothers had done something a few years back, which I had vowed that I would never forgive him for. The woman leading the Bible study group said, 'If you would like to forgive someone, just write their name down on this piece of paper' and handed round small bits of paper. I thought, 'Oh well, perhaps it's time to forgive him.' So I just wrote down, 'Brother'. Then I folded the piece of paper up and gave it in with the others. She looked at them and then led us in prayer. At the end, this black girl said to me, 'Did you forgive someone?'

And I said, 'Yeah.'

And she said, 'The Lord is going to forgive you. You are getting out of here.'

I said, 'Oh yeah.'

Two days later the prison officers came and got me and told me that all the charges had been dropped against me and that I was allowed to go. I still don't know why they did that, but I know I could have gone to prison for two years for what I did.

In February 1995, Wade and I were married in Jamaica. By then I was pregnant, and I didn't want to have the baby over there, so I came back the following August. Twelve weeks later, Wade joined me in Jersey after sorting out the immigration details. It meant that he missed the birth of our first baby, a little girl called Dara. Dara was born with several very serious heart defects, which meant that she had to have a series of operations after her birth. I was working in the local Safeway supermarket at the time, and I remember sitting at the check-out telling a friend that I was off to Southampton to be with Dara for another big operation at the hospital. Our conversation was overheard by a lady waiting in the queue for the check-out, and when it came to her turn she said, 'I overheard you talking. Why don't you bring your little girl along to our playgroup?' The lady's name was Loraine and I recognised her as someone who came to my check-out all the time, so I said, 'OK.' I asked her where it was – and it turned out to be St Paul's mums-

and-toddlers group, which was linked to St Paul's church in St Helier.

I went along just before taking Dara to Southampton and while I was there, somebody asked me about her and asked if she could pray for her. I said, 'Yes, certainly' – so she did. That was in July 1996 and Dara's operation went ahead in Southampton. At around that time, the group ended for the summer, but the following September I went back because they were so friendly. It was then that some of the other mums asked me if I might be interested in doing a course investigating Christianity on Friday mornings. It was called Alpha. I was quite keen and said, 'Yes.' By this time, our son Ben had been born, and I went along with him and Dara and we watched the videos. There were only about four or five of us doing the course, but it was fun. We had tea and coffee and cakes, watched the video and then had a discussion group. I kept Ben with me because he was tiny and slept through most of it, while there was someone there to look after Dara.

Our Alpha weekend sessions were on a Friday evening and Saturday – and I had a very tearful experience. I told somebody my story – about what happened to me in Miami – and it was like a confession kind of thing which I wanted to get out. They prayed for me, and I couldn't help feeling that God had been with me all along, getting me freed from jail and even putting Loraine in my check-out queue. Around then, I said a prayer asking God into my life. I didn't have any electric bolts run through me, but I felt a kind of peace settling on me. It was like I had finished searching and I could relax now. I had found what I was looking for. I mentioned to Wade that I wanted to go to church and he was very happy for me to go with the children, although he didn't come. He had a vast knowledge of the Bible because his mum is a Christian and they are very, very religious in Jamaica, but he's not a churchgoer himself.

I made many friends at the church who gave me great support over Dara's sickness. Dara had to go in for heart surgery in Southampton hospital in December 1997, and the consultants didn't really hold out much hope for her, because of the extent of the surgery required. She went into the operating theatre on 7 December for a long operation – and then, five days later, she was operated on again because she wasn't making any progress. She was unconscious in intensive care for five weeks after that – and then she woke up. I don't think any of them thought she would. We had been praying so much for her that it was just so exciting. Within two weeks of waking up, she was walking and talking – and on 26 January we took her home to Jersey.

But she had this cough which wasn't very good and every now and again it would get really bad. I kept taking her to Jersey Hospital, and they kept saying there wasn't anything they could do for it, as there was no infection. I asked about taking her to Southampton, but they said they didn't think it was necessary. They said she would get better soon. But she grew increasingly worse – until one day early in March when I was holding her and she looked so strange. We called an ambulance which took her to Jersey Hospital, where a doctor looked at her and said he would arrange for her to be taken to Southampton during the next few days. I was very worried because she kept vomiting. A friend telephoned Wade who turned up and Dara, who always called him Wade instead of daddy, said, 'Wade, Wade.' They were very, very close. Then I noticed a number of marks on her chest and her tummy. I called in a doctor and said, 'What are they?' but he didn't know. A little while later, a nurse brought Wade and me some coffee and as she brought it in, one of us noticed that Dara wasn't breathing.

All I remember was just screaming. For some reason I looked at my watch and it was one-thirty. Then they asked us to leave and I said that I didn't want to – but finally we did. And I think they tried to bring her round for about half an hour. But they didn't succeed. She just died. They said it was chronic heart failure, which I don't believe. I don't think I would have been able to get through all that we went through without the help of the church. They prayed with me and looked after us time and again. Nevertheless, I do blame the hospital. I had a meeting with the consultants in Southampton about six months after it happened. They said that as soon as Dara was taken to hospital that morning, she should have been put in intensive care with a nurse or a doctor with her all the time. Members of the church have prayed with me about my anger over what happened – and there is no doubt that God has done lots of wonderful things for me. He gave me Charley, our son, who was born in October 1999.

Before doing Alpha, I saw Jesus as little more than some-body who came down and performed the odd miracle. Now I believe that he went through terrible pain and died on the cross to forgive us our sins. Since becoming a Christian, my outlook has changed. I used to be quite wild, going out and doing a lot of partying. But my attitude has changed. I've nothing against partying, but I was doing it in excess and I feel now it is better done in moderation. I can still lose my temper quite a lot, but I do pray about that a lot and I find that it helps.

When I pray, I just speak to God and ask him to help me.

I feel I can talk to him about anything. He's with me all the time. Even though I lost a child, God never left us. And one day I'll find out why it happened. It's often hard and I sometimes wonder why – but my trust has never gone. That has never, ever been an issue. My belief has never wavered.

Deborah Field now helps lead the mother-and-toddler group at St Pauls where she first did the Alpha course. 'Now I help to bring other people to Jesus Christ' she said.

11

'We sold a million, but I wasn't happy . . .'

The story of Donna Matthews

As a guitarist and vocalist with Elastica, Donna Matthews hit the big time when the group's debut album went straight to number one in the UK charts. But life was not easy. Here she tells the story:

My mum and dad divorced when I was about two. Some four years after that my dad went to prison for drugs. I've got two sisters: Ceri is three years older than me and Lisa is a year younger. We grew up on a council estate, later exchanging to a village called Bishton in south Wales. Family life was good – we were really close. It was my mum and us three girls. We didn't have much money but we were quite a loving family and we'd often go and visit my dad on weekends. He was quite a long way away in prison in Dartmoor. He got moved a few times. He was in for about seven years.

My dad played guitar and was interested in music, and I think that's where I got my interest in music from. My mum used to smoke dope and at about 12 I started smoking dope too. I became really rebellious – I got into drugs and music and the whole punk culture really. Around that time my dad came out of prison and got a house in Newport, so I started going into town a lot more. Me and my sister Lisa started busking in town and through that met older boys who had bands. We'd start hanging out with them and we lost interest in school.They also had access to harder drugs and by the age of 14 I was doing acid and speed.

Sometimes I'd sit in on my own on week nights and take mushrooms or speed and then go to school the next day and sniff glue and aerosols. At that time I was self-harming as well and I got done in school for cutting my arm. I was always in trouble for everything – for truancy, for writing on the desks, for shouting at teachers, for not paying attention and for stealing stuff from the classrooms. My mum would say, 'I can't control you. You're out of control.' Sometimes she'd sit me down and say, 'Look – this has got to stop. I can't take it.'

I'd think, 'I'll try, I'll try, I'll try . . .' And then the next day I wouldn't be able to control myself.

When I was 14 the school said that I'd have to leave if I didn't behave. I said, 'Well, I'm gonna leave anyway.' And I just left.

My mum then said, 'Look, I can't take any more. You're uncontrollable. I want you to move to your dad's.'

I was like, 'Great.' I had a lot more freedom living with my dad, I was allowed to stay out late and do whatever I wanted really.

My dad was a rebel and he took drugs. He used to take

me to nightclubs and things like that. When the truancy officers called at my dad's, he would say, 'Oh, she's not staying here.'

When the authorities eventually caught up with me they put me into a special needs unit for wayward children in Hartridge, South Wales. I was 15 by then. I had a boyfriend at the time, and in the evenings I would go into Newport to see him. At 16 I was allowed to leave Hartridge and I moved into town. I didn't have any qualifications and I just started selling drugs. I started off by buying a bit of dope and selling that, and then over the next couple of years I built up a business selling dope and speed. I ended up selling kilos of dope – like nine ounce bars – and I'd buy two ounces of speed and I'd sell it in grams. I did have some proper work – menial jobs like bar work and things like that – but basically I didn't know what I wanted to do.

By this time I had sort of dropped out of society – I had dyed hair and I was in the punk rock scene. I was a bit lost. I knew I wanted to do music but I sort of lost all my confidence. I was taking a lot of acid and had a bit of a breakdown. I got really disillusioned with life and started thinking, 'What's the point of it all?' I had been writing songs since I was about ten and was still doing some music. When I was 17, I bought an electric guitar and started playing that. I'd sit playing for hours and that became my solace really. I was living with a boyfriend in Newport, just above a nightclub. Around that time I had a driving instructor who was a bit of a psychiatrist and he'd sort of counsel me a little bit. I'd say, 'Society – there's no point in it all. It's all useless. I'm into green politics.'

He'd say, 'Well, why don't you work for CND or Greenpeace?'

I'd say, 'Yeah, but it's not worth it.'

He'd say to me, 'Look, if you want to do something about a problem, you have to take action.'

Bit by bit it started sinking in, and so when I was about 18 or 19 I decided to go back to college. I thought, 'I'm gonna go back and try and get some O-levels and then do a degree.'

I started college – a tech in Newport – and made new friends. I started changing the way I dressed and looked a little bit. I then joined the college band and that was the beginning of a new era for me. I was still dealing dope but to a different crowd of people – less the sort of real manic drug heads to more like casual dope-smokers. I then started playing in another band that I'd formed. It was good and I started thinking, 'This is what I want to do.' The first band had been sort of a covers band, but the second band was Indie music like, 'The Jesus and Mary Chain', 'Pixies', 'Nirvana' – which were all around then. That band was quite successful and it started making me think. For the first time I had hope. I could see a future and I started laying the foundations for what I wanted to do. I did O-level art and then I started doing an art A-level, but I only got halfway through that and music sort of took over. There had been a few arguments in our band and I thought, 'I'm gonna go up to London and get a band together.' It was around 1990. I was 20 years old.

I'd been to London when I was younger but I didn't really have a clue. I knew of someone from Newport who'd moved to London and was in a band. So I got his number and asked if I could crash on his floor until I found somewhere to live. And that's what I did. I then started looking through the back of music papers like the *NME* and *Melody*

Maker and answered some ads and started auditioning. I auditioned for a band called 'Onk' who were looking for a guitarist. The audition was at a place called 'The Premises' down in Hackney. After half an hour they said, 'Yep – cool' – and that was it.

There were three there: bass player, Annie; the singer, Justine; and the drummer, Justin. We later changed our name to Elastica. Our first gig was about eight months later, and me and Justine wrote all the songs. A lot of Justine's were about frustration, and mine were about questioning my reality a bit. I think I was always looking at deeper meanings and things. I was still doing drugs at this stage, but not heavily – I couldn't afford it. I'd smoke a bit of dope and maybe do some speed on the weekend, but not heavy use. It was the same for the others. We started becoming successful and getting a bit more money. We were invited to more parties and the pressures grew. We would have to go from one thing to another and we were on the road a lot. We would be drinking one night and then the next day we'd be travelling again, so we'd all be drinking and then you'd take drugs to counteract the alcohol. We would end up going on benders for a couple of weeks and have a week off. Bit by bit those stretches got closer and closer together.

After a couple of years in the band – and we'd started making a lot of money quite fast – we were on a continual bender. We would get through hundreds of pounds worth of drugs in a week. I was taking heroin by then. The other band members were doing it too. We all smoked it, but I ended up getting into needles when I was about 24 or 25. Life in the band was what would be classed as glamorous. We had lots of money, we'd get planes here, there and everywhere. We'd fly to this country and that just for a party. It was like a lot of drugs and excess really, and it was supposedly fun, but bit by bit I started feeling really, really empty. I had this double life. One day I'd be out doing a TV programme or something, and the next I'd be home down the Cross [Kings Cross] hanging round with crack addicts and going back to their squats. I'd bought the flat there because it was somewhere I could get drugs 24 hours a day. The more I got into that way of living, the more I retreated from any friends and the more drugs became my friends.

In the band we became more and more unfriendly because of the stresses. We started getting into a lot of arguments and would lie to each other all the time. At this stage we were supposed to be in a studio every day recording our second album. It was like a grand a day for the studio and we'd hardly turn up. We had the studio for about two years. The first album we produced – which was just called 'Elastica' – went on and sold like a million copies. The second album took five years to make and then it dribbled out. I left the band before it came out because I didn't want any part of it really. I didn't think it was a very good album. That was in 1998.

My heroin habit then started to become really debilitating. I got to the point where I didn't really leave my bedroom. I didn't really go out and I didn't answer the phone (I was scared of the phone) – I was paranoid, I was totally fearful and incapable of living. All I could do was get up and 'use' and then I'd sleep, use, sleep, use. As well as heroin I'd be injecting speed. I'd take speed to help me get out and face the world and then gear to make me relax. I had lots of random boyfriends – no one meaningful. Around that time I had a few breakdowns where I couldn't cope. The fear just felt so extreme. One night when I'd taken heroin I even had an experience where I thought I'd gone to hell. It was a place with burning people – it was just horrible. When I came back to my room I was so scared I went straight out of my house without any shoes or socks on. I got in my car and drove to someone else's house. I was terrified. My mind started to go.

I had tried for years to get clean. I kept saying, 'I'm not going to use, I'm not going to use.' And I'd try different things to get clean, but every time I'd use again. I wanted to get clean because I knew it was killing me, and I didn't like the person I was becoming. It was stealing my soul. When I first took heroin it used to make me feel like I was in heaven. Then, as time went on, I'd feel fearful when I was taking it and even more fearful when I wasn't. Towards the end I would be absolutely beside myself with terror at facing the world when the heroin wore off. I'd feel so raw that I'd do almost anything for some heroin. I'd then take some more just to make the fear go away. It would be a relief to feel sort of normal again. I'd feel like a functioning person. I wouldn't feel high – it would just make me be able to sit in my skin. People don't keep using because they want to but because they have to. Without it, it's like having a massive mental and physical breakdown. The pain of getting clean was harder than the pain of being on it. It seemed invincible.

At 27 I decided to go back home to my mum in Wales and I was there for nearly six months – but I still couldn't get clean. I lied to my mum that I was clean and then she would find me using again. I just couldn't get back on my feet. She'd come into my bedroom and there'd be foil around me – and I'd be passed out. Soon after that I managed to get onto a treatment programme to get off the heroin. It was for eight weeks at Barley Wood in Bristol. I thought, 'This is my last chance.'

The treatment centre was horrible – about four very sick people to a room. It was a 12-step treatment centre, so it was based on having a spiritual awakening to recover. Each day would start with some sort of spiritual reading from a 12-step book. After that we'd have breakfast and then you'd have to do some Therapy Duties (TDs): cleaning, washing-up – that sort of thing. We'd also have to make our bed and tidy our room. Then we'd have an hour and a half of teaching – normally something about addiction. I felt absolute terror throughout this time. I was scared of everything and I was so ill. All the people who had recovered said that they had prayed to God and he had helped them to get clean – so I thought, 'Right, I'm going to try praying.'

One night I lay in bed and prayed. I just said, 'If there is a God and you can hear me, then please help me.' I remember being quite embarrassed when I prayed it. I then woke up in the middle of the night and thought I wanted to go to the toilet. I sat in the toilet but didn't want to go. As I sat there I thought, 'What am I doing?' I started crying – and I cried and cried for ages. I then went back to bed, and when I got up in the morning I felt like something had changed in me. That started me thinking, 'Well, if this God is real, then I'd better find out what God is.' I kept praying, 'God show me.' From then on I went on a mission to know God and I started getting better.

When I finished the programme I went to visit my family, but I couldn't handle the emotions I felt and I thought, 'I need some heroin – and I need it now.' I stole my sister's car and went to the dealer's house in Newport. The whole way in the car I was praying, 'God please help me, please help me, please help. Help me not to use.' I got to the dealer's house. The lights were on and I knocked on the door. I could see the telly on but he didn't answer the door. I shouted through the letterbox and he still didn't answer, so I had to leave and I drove back to my mum's house. I feel that God helped me that night.

After living in Bristol for about a month I returned to my flat in Kings Cross and started attending 12-step meetings about twice a day, every day. I started doing music again and wrote a few songs. I saw my old band and actually went to see them play. I got up on stage with them. I think they were really pleased that I'd got clean. On the 12-step programme you have to have a sponsor – someone who helps you through the steps. My sponsor was a Christian. She took me to church once but it didn't really mean that much. I wasn't interested. I believed that God was a higher form of consciousness – part of me, within me and in everything and everyone. It wasn't a person, it was an energy or something like that. I basically thought there were two energy forces in the universe – good and evil – and God was the good force.

Later I started attending a food addiction 12-step programme and my sponsee there turned out to be a Christian who attended a church called Holy Trinity Brompton. In 2002, someone else from the 12-step programme mentioned to me about the Alpha course at HTB and I thought, 'I'll go along.' I was quite cynical and didn't think I needed Christianity in my life. But I had two friends who were Christians and I thought they were lovely people. So I went. I missed the first night of the course and started on the second week. I went in and sat on the top balcony which was full of people. There must have been a couple of hundred people there I think. I wasn't expecting that. I thought there'd be a few sombre-faced people, but instead it was lively and exciting.

I was introduced to my group, which included a couple of people I recognised from the 12-step food programme I was in. I thought, 'Hmmm . . . Fancy seeing you here . . .' It was nice. After the supper Nicky Gumbel [Alpha course presenter] got up to speak. He seemed to really believe in what he was talking about and that inspired me. At the end of his talk, Nicky gave people a chance to say a prayer to invite Jesus into their lives. He said, 'If anyone wants to offer their lives to Christ, to get to know Christ, then just say "I'm sorry for the things I've done . . ." ' and he led people in the prayer. I said that prayer then. But despite that, I still questioned everything. I thought, 'Maybe he's deluded. I think that there's lots of paths to God and that's his, that's his truth.' It didn't make me want to change my path. In the group discussion we'd talk about things and I didn't really feel like my questions were answered, but I'd voice them anyway.

Half way through the course we went on the Alpha weekend about the Holy Spirit. I was fine with it. Sometimes if I was praying or meditating, or listening to music, I would feel a feeling of peace, joy and wholeness. I thought that was what the Holy Spirit was. The weekend was held in Pakefield, Suffolk. It was good. I liked it but I was still cynical. On the Saturday evening I was still quite cynical of everything. I thought, 'I've experienced more Spirit than you.' I was thinking I was way more spiritually advanced than the other people there. When we got to the end of the talk, the speaker invited us all to stand. He then said, 'Put your hands out – those who want to receive the Spirit.' So I held my hands out. He then invited the Holy Spirit to come. Some people started singing in tongues and suddenly I started singing in tongues. I felt like a bird. I felt like this music was coming out of my mouth.

It just happened. It felt like this beautiful voice came out – and I haven't got a beautiful voice. I felt flooded with warmth. I felt completely, completely at home. It felt like clear water was coming through me, pushing everything out of me. I started crying – sobbing and sobbing. I was still standing up but my whole body was shaking, and my friend Caroline next to me was also shaking – and that went on for quite a while. We were both sobbing. After that we then both started hugging each other. We were crying and then we started laughing. That night after the session there was a disco and I was boogie-ing on the dance floor and thinking, 'There's more to all this than I first thought . . .' I had a dream that night. There was a plant that kept floating up to the sky and the roots were all dangling, and I kept trying to press the roots into the ground but it kept floating off again.

The next day we all regrouped in the main hall and there was a reading from Ephesians. It said something about Jesus being soil that we need to plant our roots in, and then about how wide, how deep is God's love for us in Christ. I'd told Caroline about my dream and she turned to me and said, 'That's what your dream meant last night.' I'd been trying to keep the plant in the soil and it kept rising up. I realised I needed Jesus to keep me planted in reality and help me deal with the world. I said a prayer, 'Lord, forgive me for all the things I've done. I'm sorry for the things I've done in my past. I offer myself to you.' I meant it. The weekend was amazing. I still had lots of questions but I got into the course more after that.

A good few weeks after the Alpha course had ended I

started drifting back into thinking, 'Oh well, I don't really need to become a Christian.' I then happened to speak to someone in the 12-step programme who was a Christian and she said, 'How's it going, becoming a Christian?'

I said, 'Well, you know, I don't really know if I'm supposed to become a Christian or not.'

She said, 'Well, just keep praying and asking God.'

I said, 'Oh I've been doing that.'

Then I remembered that I'd had this little leaflet come through the door, which said, 'God will help you . . . Jesus is God's way. The Bible says in John 3:16–17: "For God so loved the world that he gave his one and only Son, that whoever believes in him shall not perish but have eternal life. For God did not send his Son into the world to condemn the world, but to save the world through him." ' And I told her this.

She said, 'Oh – my father died recently. We held his funeral last week and that was the reading on his grave-stone.' She then said God sometimes speaks to us through these coincidences.

The following day when I opened my Bible I happened to open it up at John 3:16. I had randomly put the leaflet in my Bible as a bookmark, but I had put it on exactly the same page. I was like, 'OK. That's too weird.' I went to church the next day and the reading was the same reading. I thought, 'God is definitely trying to tell me something . . .' So I joined a pastorate at HTB. That was last October [2002]. After that I kept praying to Jesus to show me the right way, and basically my relationship with Jesus has just been grow-ing since then. I definitely had a relationship with God before, but now it's more intensified with Jesus. It's like the road that I'm on there's more light. I read the Bible every day now and its wisdom touches my soul and keeps me growing and learning. Some of the Old Testament I find a bit bizarre, but I just keep reading and praying for God to help me understand.

In January 2003 I got baptised, and I would say that was when I properly became a Christian. I had been going to HTB for six months and knew how much it was changing my life. I thought I had to make a commitment.

When I think of my past now I think it's all quite dark. I don't know what the future holds, but I have God to help me.

Donna remains a member of Holy Trinity Brompton. She says: 'God has removed completely my desire for drugs and alcohol . . . My desire now is to know God and to serve God.'

If you are interested in finding out more about the
Christian faith and would like to be put in touch with
your nearest Alpha course, please see:

alphacourse.org

Or contact:
The Alpha Office, Holy Trinity Brompton,
Brompton Road, London SW7 1JA
Tel: 0845 644 7533 Fax: 020 7052 0204
Email: info@alphacourse.org

The God Who Changes Lives
Volume One, Two & Three

Edited by Mark Elsdon-Dew

Does God act in people's lives today?

Three volumes of stories from people whose lives have been dramatically touched by an encounter with God. Some tell of restored relationships; others how they have been given strength in the midst of pain.

These are books for anyone interested in whether God is there – and what he can do.

Alpha – Questions of Life by Nicky Gumbel

What is the point of life?
What happens when we die?
Is forgiveness possible?
Who is Jesus?
What relevance does he have for our lives today?

In 15 compelling chapters Nicky Gumbel tackles the
answers to these and other key questions, pointing the way
to an authentic Christianity that is exciting and relevant to
today's world.

'*Alpha – Questions of Life* is a sympathetic, fascinating
and immensely readable introduction to Jesus Christ – still
the most attractive and captivating person that it is possible
to know. Nicky Gumbel's informed approach ensures that
the search for truth fully engages our minds as well as our
hearts.'

– From the foreword by SANDY MILLAR

Why Jesus? by Nicky Gumbel

Many people today are puzzled about Jesus.

Why is there so much interest in a person born nearly 2,000 years ago?
Why are so many people excited about Jesus?
Why do we need him? Why did he come? Why did he die?
Why should anyone bother to find out?

Nicky Gumbel tackles these issues in *Why Jesus?* a challenging, short presentation of Jesus Christ.

Nicky Gumbel practised as a barrister and is now ordained and on the staff of Holy Trinity Brompton, London.

These publications are available from your local Christian bookshop or contact:

Alpha Publications Hotline for telephone orders:
0845 758 1278 (all calls at local rates)

To order from overseas:
Tel: +44 1228 611 749
Fax: +44 1228 514 949
alpha@stl.org